SCHOLASTIC

The Primary Teacher's Guide to
Religious Education

• Key subject knowledge • Background information • Teaching tips •

Dr Geoff Teece

■SCHOLASTIC

Book End, Range Road, Witney, Oxfordshire, OX29 0YD
www.scholastic.co.uk
© 2012 Scholastic Ltd
1 2 3 4 5 6 7 8 9   2 3 4 5 6 7 8 9 0 1

British Library Cataloguing-in-Publication Data
A catalogue record for this book is available from the
British Library.

ISBN 978-1407-12781-1
Printed and bound by CPI Group (UK) Ltd, Croydon,
CR0 4YY.

Due to the nature of the web, we cannot guarantee
the content or links of any site mentioned. We strongly
recommend that teachers check websites before using
them in the classroom.

Author
Geoff Teece

Commissioning Editor
Paul Naish

Development Editor
Pollyanna Poulter

Proofreader
Kate Manson

Indexer
Penny Brown

Illustration
Garry Davies

Icons
Tomek.gr

Series Designers
Shelley Best and Sarah Garbett

Acknowledgements

Every effort has been made to trace copyright
holders for the works reproduced in this book,
and the publishers apologise for any inadvertent
omissions.

About the author

Dr Geoff Teece was previously director of the
Westhill RE Centre and is now lecturer in RE at
the University of Birmingham.

Author acknowledgements

I would like to thank many people in the religious
communities of Birmingham who I have been
privileged to know for so many years and who have
taught me so much. In particular: Padmakumara,
Mahasiddhi and Alokavira of the Birmingham
Buddhist Centre; Deseta Davies of The Church of
God of Prophecy, Aberdeen Street; Ruth Jacobs
of Pershore Road Orthodox Synagogue; Father
Alexander Zebic of St Lazars Serbian Orthodox
Church, Bournville; Mr Sharma Dvividi of Shree
Geeta Bhawan Mandir, Handsworth; Bhai Sahib,
Bhai Mohinder Singh Ji, Ramandeep Kaur and Pripal
Kaur Riat of Guru Nanak Nishkam Sewak Jatha;
Mr Mohammad Ali, Dr Mohammad Naseem,
Ch. Abdul Rashid and Imam Hafiz Ahmed Ibrahim
Patel of Birmingham Central Mosque. Finally, special
thanks to the late Professor John Hick for his
inspiration and kindness.

Contents

Introduction 5

Chapter 1 Buddhism 9

Chapter 2 Christianity 34

Chapter 3 Hinduism 68

Chapter 4 Islam 103

Chapter 5 Judaism 139

Chapter 6 Sikhism 174

Glossary 210

Index 221

Icon key

Information within this book is highlighted in the margins by a series of different icons. They are:

Subject facts
Key subject knowledge is clearly presented and explained in this section.

Why you need to know these facts
Provides justification for understanding the facts that have been explained in the previous section.

Vocabulary
A list of key words, terms and language relevant to the preceding section. Vocabulary entries appear in the glossary.

Sensitive issues
Highlights areas that require consideration before presentation to the class, including personal, social and cultural issues.

Amazing facts
Interesting snippets of background knowledge to share.

Common misconceptions
Identifies and corrects some of the common misconceptions and beliefs that may be held about the subject area.

Teaching ideas
Outlines practical teaching suggestions using the knowledge explained in the preceding section.

Religious Education

The *Primary Teacher's Guide to Religious Education* is designed to enable primary teachers to become more effective practitioners of religious education. Of course to be an effective teacher of RE is a complex and demanding task. A good RE teacher understands the nature and aims of the subject and is able to put this understanding into practice. Unlike other subjects, RE is not governed by a nationally prescribed curriculum. Rather it is part of the basic curriculum and is subject to the requirements of a locally agreed syllabus.

Effective RE

In recent times, these syllabuses have reflected a growing consensus about the nature of RE. Although expressed in different ways, most agreed syllabuses place an emphasis on three distinct but interrelated areas of study, namely that RE should enable pupils:

- to develop a knowledge and understanding of religion
- to explore fundamental questions arising out of our shared human experience of life
- to learn from religion and human experience, so developing their own ideas, beliefs and values and becoming more mature and intelligent in their thinking about religion.

In this way pupils should be able to develop an ability to ask relevant questions not only about religion but also draw on what they have learnt about religion to ask critical questions about the world in which they live. So, for example, a topic on the Creation story in Christianity for Year 6 pupils may challenge them to ask questions about the Biblical account: *Is it true? What does being 'true' mean?* However, really effective RE will also enable them to take what they have learned about Christian views of creation, such as the importance of human **stewardship** of the Earth, and ask questions about human behaviour such as: *Do we treat the Earth properly? Whose world is it?*

The focus of this book

To encompass all these elements in a book such as this is a difficult and, perhaps, impossible task, and no attempt has been made here to offer a fully comprehensive guide to the RE curriculum. Choices had to be made and it was decided to concentrate largely on providing the reader with some basic and reliable knowledge of the six major religious traditions that are represented in local agreed syllabuses for RE. Most non-specialist teachers know that this is an area in which they need the most help. A teacher can hardly be expected to fully realise the aims for the subject without a reasonable knowledge of what he or she is expected to teach. The original edition of this book, published in 2001, proved popular with non-specialist RE teachers, at both primary and secondary, for precisely this reason. Consequently, the basic structure of the original book has been maintained with appropriate updating where necessary.

Of course a book such as this cannot inform the reader about everything there is to know about the world's religions and, arguably, teachers can't and don't need to know everything there is to know. It is more important that teachers are enabled to develop skills and ways of understanding that help them make sense of religious belief and practice.

The nature of the religions

Therefore, whilst the main aim of the book is to provide the reader with a sound understanding of some key and professionally relevant aspects of each religion, it also seeks to go beyond the mere presentation of information. An attempt has been made to present each religion in such a way that each makes sense to the reader in the context of the aims and process of RE as outlined on page 5. This has meant taking a particular view about what role religions play in people's lives. Arguably, religions provide two very important things for their followers.

First, religions provide an analysis of human nature and they all portray human nature as being in some way incomplete or unsatisfactory. The Western Semitic traditions of Judaism,

Christianity and Islam tend to see this unsatisfactoriness in largely moral terms; that there is, in human nature, a natural inclination to fall away from God, whether it is through sin in Christianity, evil inclination in Judaism or forgetfulness and self-centredness in Islam. In the religions that developed in India, namely Buddhism, Hinduism and Sikhism, the focus is on false consciousness leading to ignorance and spiritual blindness.

Second, religions provide not only an analysis of human imperfection but also a 'path' or 'way' to enable the believer to transcend this imperfect nature and in doing so become more fully human. Of course each religion differs as to what this 'goal' of life is. It might be the eternal life lived in the kingdom of God for the Christian or the 'blowing out' of desire and craving and hence an end to suffering for the Buddhist who seeks **nibbana** or *nirvana*. Religions are, in the words of Professor Ninian Smart, 'systems of salvation'.

Because religions have this interpretive role in the lives of people, an attempt has been made in each chapter to place the information about religious beliefs and practices within the context of how members of each faith understand the nature of human salvation or liberation. In most cases this is seen in the relationship between humanity and God, the exception being Buddhism, which stresses human effort committed to the eternal **dhamma**, taught by Buddha, as the way to *nibbana*.

The structure of the book

Each chapter of the book follows a common pattern. The sections in each chapter are based on areas of study recommended by many agreed syllabuses for RE. For each section basic **Subject facts** are given as well as **Why you need to know these facts** and their importance in the context of RE teaching. The **Common misconceptions** sections deal with perceived fallacies as well as attempting to answer common questions that teachers may have about the subject matter. **Sensitive issues** are dealt with where appropriate and a **Vocabulary** list is given for each section. This is expanded to a glossary, which you can find at the end of the book, with definitions listed by religion, as a quick reference guide. At the end of each section there is a list of **Teaching ideas**. These ideas are not intended to be fully worked out activities but to act as an initial stimulus for teaching about the particular aspect of the religion concerned. Each chapter also includes a brief list of **Resources**, which recommends relevant visual materials and artefacts, books and websites.

Dates

Religious communities measure time differently. For example, the Christian calendar determines its dates from the time of Jesus, and the Muslim calendar from the Hijrah, the journey of the Prophet Muhammad to Makkah in 622CE. In order not to give offence to any religious communities, the dates given in this book are based on the Gregorian calendar. The terms BCE (Before the Common Era) and CE (the Common Era), correspond to the Christian terms BC and AD, respectively.

Buddhism

Buddhism originated in North-East India sometime between the 6th and 4th centuries BCE with the historical figure known as Buddha. About 250 years after Buddha, Buddhism began to spread around India during the reign of the Emperor Asoka. As a convert, Emperor Asoka was so keen to see Buddhism spread around the world that he sent monks to Sri Lanka, Nepal and Tibet. The religion spread to places like China and Thailand and at one time a third of the world's population was Buddhist. As Buddhism spread worldwide, it took on the culture and folk religion of each new country it arrived in. This can confuse travellers from the West who cannot see much of a connection between the Buddhism in Sri Lanka and the Buddhism in Japan. However, whatever cultural forms Buddhism might take, the **dhamma** (the teachings as exemplified by Buddha) remain constant.

The spread of the religion has resulted in several different schools of Buddhism. The oldest form is called Theravada (way of the elders). Theravada Buddhists believe that they follow a path closest to the words of Buddha. They also regard vinaya (living a monastic life) as the best path to enlightenment and Theravada monks can be recognized by their saffron-coloured robes. This form can be found in Sri Lanka and South-East Asia and hence is sometimes referred to as 'southern' Buddhism.

Buddhism also spread north from India to Tibet and Japan. In such countries as these, people follow a form of Buddhism called Mahayana (the 'great way' or 'career'). This emphasises compassion in the form of the bodhisattva (wisdom being) – one who is destined for enlightenment but who, out of compassion, postpones his or her final attainment of Buddhahood in order to help others. This form includes Zen Buddhism and Pure Land Buddhism.

Another form, called Vajrayana (the diamond way), spread from India to Tibet around 700CE. Some call this form Tantric Buddhism because it was influenced by the tantra, a movement in which meditation is accompanied by complicated rituals. Their maroon robes can easily identify Tibetan monks and nuns. Perhaps the most famous Tibetan Buddhist is the Dalai Lama, who is the head of a particular Tibetan Buddhist tradition.

It is estimated that there are around 376 million Buddhists in the world today and some 152,000 in Britain. Most forms of Buddhism can be found in the West and in more recent years a Western Buddhist movement called The Friends of the Western Buddhist Order has flourished. This movement encompasses aspects of the other schools of Buddhism but is dedicated to practising the dhamma in a way that is suited to Western culture. This chapter provides an introduction to three areas of study: Buddha, dhamma (Buddhist teaching) and **sangha** (the Buddhist community). These three aspects are usually referred to as the Three Jewels.

Siddhattha Gotama, Buddha

Subject facts

The Buddha's birth and early life

Siddhattha Gotama, Buddha, was born in India about 2500 years ago. He was born into the Shakya clan from the Kshatriya (warrior) caste. Consequently, he is also referred to as Shakyamuni, 'the Shakya sage'. His father was King Shudhodana Gotama; his mother, Queen Maya. His joyous father named him Siddhattha (every wish fulfilled).

Before Siddhattha was born, his mother had a dream about a white elephant. This was thought to signify that her son would grow up to be someone very special. Siddhattha is said to have been born when his mother stopped to rest in a beautiful grove called Lumbini. At his birth, a wise man told Shudhodana Gotama that his son would grow up to be a powerful king if he was kept away from the sorrows and reality of life. However, if Siddhattha did learn about or see the sorrows and reality of life, he would grow up to be a great universal teacher. His father wanted his son to be happy and so pledged to keep his son shielded from real life. Consequently, as a child Siddhattha was not allowed to leave the palace grounds.

The Buddha's search for happiness

When he grew up, Siddhattha married a beautiful young princess called Yasodhara and she gave birth to a son called Rahula. The young man Siddhattha was rich and he had a beautiful wife and son – everything he could want. But the pleasures of married life did not distract Siddhattha for long. He was restless and longed to experience something more than just the insides of the palace grounds.

One day he persuaded his charioteer, Chanda, to take him for a drive outside the palace. What he saw was to change his life. They are known as the four sights. Firstly, he saw an old wrinkled man; he was horrified to realise that he too would become old and wrinkled. Next, he saw a sick person, obviously in great pain; again Siddhattha was shocked to realise that he too could become ill. The third sight was that of a dead person and Siddhattha realised that we all get sick, we all grow old and we all have to die. Such unhappiness upset Siddhattha. On his way back to the palace he saw his fourth sight – a man who looked happy. He was wearing the saffron robes of a monk. The monk lived a simple life searching for the meaning of existence.

These sights so disturbed Siddhattha that instead of applying himself to his princely duties, he continually thought about the problems and causes of suffering. One night when Siddhattha was 29, he and Chanda left the palace once more. Coming to the edge of a forest, Siddhattha cut off his hair and put on simple clothes. He sent his rich clothes back to the palace with Chanda.

Siddhattha decided to find someone who could teach him how to be free from suffering and could answer the questions that had been occupying his mind. Remembering the monk and how happy he looked, Siddhattha visited ascetic teachers to find answers to his questions. The ascetics told him that since owning things didn't make him happy he should give them up and live the life of a mendicant monk. He practised severe fasting and was accompanied by five friends. However, on the point of starvation, he decided to give up this way of life; his friends were upset and left him. But Siddhattha had learnt a valuable lesson – neither great riches nor great poverty and hunger had made him happy or answered his questions. He decided that there must be a 'middle way'.

Enlightenment

Siddhattha decided to sit under a **bodhi tree** and meditate until he realized the truth. He went into deep meditation. In this state he remembered many former existences and reached a state of complete wisdom and understanding – he became enlightened. From this time, Siddhattha became known as Buddha (enlightened one). Enlightenment was not only knowing the truth in his mind, it was knowing it at such a deep level that Buddha became filled with great compassion for all beings.

So Buddha walked from **Gaya**, where he became enlightened, to Sarnath near **Varanasi**. He found his five friends sitting under a tree in the deer park there. When they saw him they could see that he had changed. Buddha preached his first sermon at the deer park and his friends became his followers, as did his family. For 35 years he taught the **dhamma** (the eternal truth) to crowds across North-East India. Many people became his followers.

When Buddha reached the age of 80, he knew that it was time for him to die. He called his followers to him and asked them if they had any questions about his teaching. His last words to his followers were, 'All things change. Keep up your effort.'

Why you need to know these facts

For Buddhists, the Buddha is not a god, or even a prophet, but a human being, albeit a special one. His life story is important because it recounts how the young man grappled with the truth of 'how things really are'. He realized his own potential and became enlightened. Buddhists believe that all people have the potential to do this and Buddha is the supreme example. It is said that when he was sitting under the bodhi tree, Buddha looked out over a pool of **lotus plants**. Some lotuses were stuck in the mud of the pool, some had buds on them and others were fully opened and clear of the water. So Buddha likened these plants to people in various stages of enlightenment. The fully opened lotus is like a person who is ready to receive the dhamma.

Vocabulary

Bodhi tree – the tree under which Buddha attained enlightenment.
Dhamma – universal law or eternal truth; for Buddhists, the
teachings that had remained hidden for years and that Buddha
'uncovered' and passed on.
Gaya – a town in North-East India. Nearby is Bodh Gaya, which
marks the place where Buddha became enlightened. It is now a
place of pilgrimage for Buddhists.
Lotus plant – a traditional Indian symbol of enlightenment.
Varanasi – holy Hindu city on the River Ganges.

Sensitive issues

There is always the potential for some children to be uncomfortable
when exploring aspects of life involving happiness and unhappiness.
It would be easier just to learn the story of Siddhattha, but don't
let the delicate nature of the topic put you off taking the discussion
further. The rule is, know your class and work from there.

Amazing facts

Siddhattha Gotama was the latest in a line of Buddhas. He did
not 'make up' his teachings, but achieved understanding of the
truth through countless lives of spiritual effort, as recorded in the
jataka tales. The dhamma did not begin with him – it is eternal,
and every enlightened being can realise it. Buddhists believe that
sometimes this truth is forgotten until another person becomes
enlightened and preaches the truth as Siddhattha did.

Common misconceptions

● There can be confusion over the names of Buddha. Buddha's
personal name was Siddhattha Gotama; the title Buddha refers to
anyone who becomes enlightened.

● Buddha is usually referred to as the founder of Buddhism. This is true in the sense that the forms of Buddhism in the world today can be traced back to the Buddha. However, it can also be misleading because, as we have already noted, the teachings are believed to be eternal.

● It is sometimes said that Buddhism is a philosophy rather than a religion, because some people believe that Buddha denied God's existence. In fact he did not. Buddha taught that enlightenment and salvation came through one's own efforts and that no one else, including a god, can do this. Buddha taught that being concerned about God and his existence was a distraction from the path of enlightenment. It is probably true to say that what makes Buddhism a religion is that it stresses the need for human beings to transcend their imperfections.

Teaching ideas

● Discuss with the children what the four sights might be if they were to see them today.

● Get the children to write about the things that make them happy. Discuss whether they think that what they have chosen will always make them happy.

The Four Noble Truths

Subject facts

All things change

What was it that Buddha realised when he became enlightened? Why is it that human beings suffer? The clue to these questions can be found in his last words to his followers, 'All things change.'

Buddha taught that everything in life changes, for example the people we love change or the job we enjoy doing changes. This is called **annica** (impermanence). Some critics of Buddhism believe that this focus on good things passing makes Buddhism a negative religion.

However, defenders of Buddism point out that all things and states are impermanent including bad things like war, pain or sadness.

Nevertheless, this awareness of annica is a major cause of suffering. The Buddhist word for this suffering is **dukkha**, which is best translated as 'unsatisfactory' rather than 'suffering' because the word 'suffering' can make us think of things like death, tragedy and illness. Whilst these are real examples of human suffering, dukkha means much more. Even happy times are the cause of suffering because they don't last. Think of the beauty of the colours of autumn or the joy of the baby born into the family. Poets often describe autumn as a melancholy season because inevitably the leaves will fall and winter will follow. Many parents feel an enormous sense of loss when their 'baby' grows up and leaves home.

Such potentially good things in life cause humans to suffer because of **tanha** (desire or craving). In short, we suffer because we want things and we want good things to last. We haven't got the money or the looks so we suffer. We want to hold on to our youth and our lives, but we can't so we suffer.

These are some of the things that Buddha came to realise when sitting under the bodhi tree. They formed the core of Buddha's first sermon at **Sarnath** known as the sermon of the Four Noble Truths.

The Four Noble Truths

One way of thinking about the Four Noble Truths might be to think in terms of human beings suffering from an illness or disease, as shown in the box below:

> **The first truth** is the illness or suffering, dukkha. Life is unsatisfactory because of the suffering and unhappiness we all feel sometimes.
> **The second truth** is the reason for the disease or suffering and this is tanha. Human beings suffer because of attachments to things that don't last.
> **The third truth** that the Buddha taught is that there is a cure to this suffering.
> **The fourth truth** is that the cure lies in following the Noble Eightfold Path, also called the 'middle way' because Buddha followed a path between hardship and luxury.

Nibbana

Understanding the Four Noble Truths and following the **Eightfold Path** helps Buddhists to achieve their goal of **nibbana** or *nirvana*, which means 'blowing out'. This is a 'blowing out' of what Buddhists call the 'three fires' or 'poisons': ignorance, hatred and greed. These poisons are the result of our craving for things. In order to reach nibbana humans have to extinguish these poisons from their nature.

Why you need to know these facts

Buddhists believe that enlightenment cannot be fully described in words, it has to be experienced. Nevertheless, the Four Noble Truths are the foundation of Buddhist teachings because they communicate the essence of what Buddha realized when he achieved enlightenment.

Vocabulary

Annica – impermanence.
Dukkha – suffering, unsatisfactoriness. According to Buddhism the basic disease of human nature from which humans need to be liberated.
Eightfold Path – guiding principles for the practice of Buddhism, with three aspects: wisdom, ethics and mental effort.
Nibbana – 'blowing out' of human desire and delusion; a state of purity and non-attachment to the 'three poisons' ignorance, hatred and greed.
Sarnath – the deer park six miles outside the holy city of Varanasi, India, where Buddha preached his first sermon.
Tanha – desire or craving. The cause of suffering.

Amazing facts

There is a legend that when Siddhattha was in deep meditation under the bodhi tree, he was visited by Mara, a satanic figure. Mara's role was to maintain ignorance and desire and to tempt Siddhattha to abandon his quest for enlightenment. Fearful that

Siddhattha was about to discover the way out of suffering, Mara sent all kinds of demons to distract him. However, Siddhattha remained concentrated and still and eventually Mara and his demons went off defeated.

Common misconceptions

Some people might think that a person could only reach nibbana when they die. This is not the case. Achieving nibbana means that because those human characteristics that cause us to suffer are extinguished there is nothing left to keep us being reborn. Nibbana means that a person becomes free of the wheel of rebirth.

Teaching ideas

● Set up a nature table in the classroom with fresh flowers and observe how they wither and die. Discuss with the children how things change and why. Do all things change?
● Get the children to bring in photographs of themselves when they were babies. Are they now the same person?
● Collect newspaper articles on suffering and explore the reasons for this. Get the children to make a list of types of suffering and to write about times when they have suffered.

The Eightfold Path

Subject facts

All Buddhists strive to follow the Eightfold Path. The path involves three aspects: wisdom, ethics and mental effort.

Wisdom
Buddhists should cultivate Right Understanding and Right Thought or Emotion. Right Understanding comes first because we cannot progress unless we see life as it really is. That means

understanding life in terms of the Four Noble Truths (see page 15). Right Thought or Emotion involves cultivating unselfishness and compassion for others. It also means that it is no use wanting to become enlightened unless the person is prepared to commit him or herself to Buddhist practice and teaching.

Ethics

Buddhists should cultivate Right Speech, Right Action and Right Livelihood. Right Speech involves telling the truth and speaking kindly and gently. Sometimes the truth can hurt so gentle speech is essential. The essential thing is not to do harm with one's speech. The basis of Right Action is good intention. A positive and compassionate state of mind is the key. Right Action involves living a life governed by the Five Precepts (see page 21). The third ethical dimension is Right Livelihood. One cannot hope to practise the Eightfold Path if your working life is in conflict with Buddhist principles. Therefore, a Buddhist's occupation must not exploit people or the planet; it must contribute towards justice and should be of benefit to others.

Mental effort

Buddhists should practise Right Effort, Right Mindfulness and Right Concentration. Discipline of the mind is essential for a happy and purposeful life. During any day we can find our mood swings from happy to sad, from approachable to aloof, from calm to angry. Right Effort involves being aware of the mental state we are in and doing something to change negative mental states into positive ones. The way to ensure this is to develop Right Mindfulness. We so often do not experience the present moment. We worry about the future, we regret things from the past, we rush to get jobs done, and we try to do too many things at once. This all leads to stress and unhappiness. Right Mindfulness involves making the most of each moment.

The key to these positive mental states is Right Concentration; some Buddhists would say Right Meditation. All Buddhists practise meditation. It is the basis of living what Buddhists call a 'more skilful' life. Meditation can take many forms but the purpose is to train the mind to become calm and positive.

The Eightfold Path also gives Buddhists their most recognisable symbol, the eight-spoked dhamma wheel, the **dhammachakra** (see Figure 1).

Figure 1

The DHAMMACHAKRA

Why you need to know these facts

Buddha taught the Four Noble Truths to explain about the causes of human suffering. The Eightfold Path is about the practice of Buddhism and is a guide to how to overcome desire and suffering. It is also essential to understanding the point of meditation for Buddhists.

Vocabulary

Dhammachakra – a wheel symbol, with eight spokes representing the Eightfold Path of Bhuddism; like the dhamma – the 'eternal truth' – the wheel has neither a beginning nor an end.

Sensitive issues

There are great benefits to be had even from very simple meditation but beware of prejudice. Some parents may be suspicious of motives. Some schools use meditation as a matter of course and claim that many benefits accrue from it in terms of a happier and calmer atmosphere. Always be very open about what you are doing.

Amazing facts

In Chinese Buddhism, the eating of garlic and onions is avoided because they are thought to heat the blood and so make meditation more difficult.

Common misconceptions

Some textbooks illustrate the Eightfold Path as consisting of eight separate steps. This can be misleading, if it is assumed that one step follows the other. Living life as a Buddhist involves them all at the same time. It is better to think of the traditional symbol of the dhammachakra – each spoke is important in the turning of the wheel.

Teaching ideas

● Get the children to think of something that they want to achieve in life and then describe eight steps to achieving it.
● Hold a class discussion on what an eightfold path for a good pupil in school might consist of. Compile the ideas into a collaborative eightfold path. Present it in an assembly.
● Visit a local Buddhist centre where there is a meditation teacher. If possible, take part in a short samatha meditation.
● Look at the concept of 'doing the right thing'. Discuss how we know what this is. Is doing the right thing enough? Do we have to have the right reason as well?

The Five Precepts

Subject facts

The Five Precepts are the foundation of Buddhist ethics. They are a guide for living and a basis for forming positive attitudes of mind. Each precept has two aspects: behaviour to be avoided; behaviour to be cultivated. Buddhists try to follow these and chant them regularly:

> **The Five Precepts**
> - Abstaining from harming any living thing and cultivating deeds of **metta** (loving kindness).
> - Abstaining from taking what has not been given and cultivating open-handed generosity.
> - Abstaining from sexual misconduct and cultivating a state of simplicity and contentment.
> - Abstaining from telling lies or speaking unkindly and cultivating truthful communication.
> - Abstaining from all intoxicants and cultivating a clear and pure mind.

Kamma

The law of **kamma**, or karma, states that all of our actions have consequences. If we become attached to the things the Five Precepts teach against we will reap unhappiness and suffering. We will also make the world as a whole a more unsatisfactory place. Through kamma we will continue to be born into the world of **samsara** (a continual round of birth, sickness, old age and death). However, by following the Eightfold Path and the Five Precepts, Buddhists believe that humans can escape samsara and achieve nibbana (see page 16).

Why you need to know these facts

All religions have an ethical dimension. Learning about the Five Precepts not only enables children to learn about an essential aspect of being a Buddhist, it enables them to think about what moral values are important to them. It also enables the children to compare these rules for living with those of other religious traditions.

Vocabulary

Kamma – action; intentional actions that affect one's circumstances in this and future lives.

Metta – loving kindness; love that is not possessive.

Samsara – the continual round of birth, sickness, old age and death.

Vinaya – the rules of discipline of monastic life.

Sensitive issues

The Clear Vision Trust suggests that the third precept could be presented as 'abstaining from being greedy'. This not only overcomes the hesitations that teachers may have about dealing with sexual misconduct but also, arguably, makes the precept more relevant to primary children.

Amazing facts

In addition to the Five Precepts, Buddhist monks and nuns follow **vinaya**. These rules for monastic life include five other precepts for novice monks: eating only one meal a day before noon, abstaining from wearing perfume and jewellery, abstaining from entertainment, abstaining from possessing money and abstaining from sleeping on a luxurious bed. Fullyfledged monks and nuns observe 227 precepts!

Common misconceptions

It would be wrong to refer to the Five Precepts as commandments. The temptation when teaching is to compare them with something like the Ten Commandments of Judaism and Christianity. Whilst there is a connection in terms of rules for living, the Precepts, unlike the Commandments, are not laid down by God. They are, rather, a set of rules for living and training that are taken on voluntarily by Buddhists. Buddhists practise the precepts in order to become like Buddha.

Teaching ideas

● Discuss with the children five rules for when they are (a) in the school, (b) in the classroom and (c) at home. These rules must be designed to make the world a better place and must have a positive 'do' as well as a negative 'don't'.
● Get the children to write a story of their own, perhaps from their own experience, that illustrates one of the positive aspects of the Precepts.

The Pali Canon

Subject facts

The **Pali Canon**, or tipitaka, is the most complete and earliest collection of Buddhist scriptures. It contains rules of the monastic discipline, teachings of Buddha and an analysis of the doctrines of Buddhism. The Pali Canon was collected and written down in Pali in Ceylon (now Sri Lanka) in the 1st century BCE.

The discourses or teachings of Buddha contained in the scriptures include many illustrations of the dhamma. These can be accessible for teaching purposes, especially in the form of stories. One such famous story, the story of Kisagotami, sometimes called 'The Mustard Seeds' or 'The Poppy Seeds', delivers the clear message that death is inevitable and emphasises the importance for Buddhists of seeing life as it really is.

The story of Kisagotami
Kisagotami lived in a village in India. She got married at a young age and had a son. She thought that she had all she needed; then, one day, tragedy struck and her husband died. She was very upset, especially as he was so young. She comforted herself with the fact that she still had her son. Then tragedy struck again. The baby got ill and eventually died. Kisagotami was devastated.

Kisagotami couldn't accept that the baby was dead and frantically sought out some medicine that could cure her son. She went from house to house asking neighbours if they had any medicine to cure her baby. She went to the doctor and he couldn't help. However, he remembered that the Buddha was staying nearby and suggested that Kisagotami visit him. The doctor told Kisagotami that because of his great wisdom Buddha might be able to help.

Buddha was sitting in the shade of a tree talking to his followers when Kisagotami approached him. He could see she was distressed and asked if he could help. She told Buddha about the sad death of her baby and that she had come to see him to ask if he could help. Buddha looked at the poor dead child and said to Kisagotami, 'In order to cure your child you must go and find some poppy seeds. Go and find four or five poppy seeds but only from a house that has never had a person die.'

Kisagotami went from house to house. Everyone could find some seeds for her but when she asked if anyone had ever died in the house the answer was always the same: death had affected someone connected with the family. In some cases it was quite recently, in others a long time ago. Whatever the case, Kisagotami could find no house where death had never entered.

Kisagotami realised that she would never get the seeds. She looked at her poor baby, said goodbye and buried him. In the evening she returned to Buddha and in his presence she grew calmer. Buddha asked if she had found any poppy seeds. 'No,' she said. 'There is no house where a loved one has not been lost. I now realize that everyone loses his or her loved ones eventually.' She had come to know just how things are in life. Everything changes and eventually dies. Kisagotami became one of Buddha's followers.

Why you need to know these facts

 The story of Kisagotami teaches in a simple way an essential truth of Buddhism – that death is inevitable. As well as the Pali Canon, look at the **jataka tales** – perhaps the richest source of stories. These stories illustrate many of the Buddhist moral perfections, such as generosity, patience, wisdom, renunciation, compassion and virtuous conduct.

Vocabulary

Jataka tales – 'birth story' tales; tales of the former lives of Buddha.
Pali Canon – the earliest and most complete form of Buddhist scriptures; also called the 'three baskets'.

Amazing facts

There are 500 or so jataka tales. Jataka means 'birth story' and each of these tales recalls an incident in one of the previous lives of Buddha. Because in many past lives Buddha was born into the animal kingdom, many of these tales are animal stories, albeit focusing on an animal or bird of unusual wisdom! There are great similarities between the jataka tales and the fables of Aesop.

Teaching ideas

Read a selection of Buddhist stories to illustrate key Buddhist values. Some good ones to concentrate on are:
- The Monkey King (self-sacrifice)
- Siddhattha and the Swan (compassion and kindness)
- The Parrot and the Fig Tree (selfless loyalty)
- The Lion and the Jackal (friendship, trust and generosity)
- The Proud Peacock and the Mallard (humility and pride)

The Sangha

Subject facts

When a person becomes a Buddhist, they make a commitment in the words of the Three Jewels or Three Refuges. These are: *I take refuge in the Buddha, I take refuge*

in the dhamma, I take refuge in the sangha. The sangha is the Buddhist community and is made up of two groups: monks and nuns, and 'lay' members.

Both monastic and 'lay' orders began at the time of Buddha when some of his early followers decided to give up their family lives to travel around and spread the dhamma. These first monks and nuns were called **bhikkhus** and **bhikkunis** respectively. Following the example of Buddha, they shaved their heads and wore a saffron yellow robe. Other Buddhists chose not to become monks or nuns, but stayed with their families and practised the teachings. They supported the bhikkhus and bhikkunis with food and became the 'lay' members of the sangha.

Today, the various forms of Buddhism understand the meaning of sangha differently. Historically, the sangha usually referred only to ordained members (monks and nuns) of the Buddhist community but today, some groups, like The Friends of the Western Buddhist Order, place little emphasis on monks and nuns and class all members of the Order as being part of the sangha; some Buddhists take 'sangha' to refer to all sentient beings with the potential for enlightenment.

In many Buddhist communities in Britain today there may be resident or visiting monks. Monks and nuns are not allowed to earn money and, as in the early days of Buddhism, the lay members of the community care for their material needs. This enables the lay people to practise **dana** (generosity). They in turn can go to the monks for their wisdom and advice.

All Buddhists promise to follow the Five Precepts (see page 21) but monks and nuns follow 227 rules for living.

Why you need to know these facts

Traditional Buddhist teaching says that a single Buddha appears only once in every 320,000 years. Siddhattha Gotama is the Buddha of our age. The sangha therefore takes on the important role of keeping alive the dhamma.

Vocabulary

Bhikkhus – Buddhist monks.
Bhikkunis – Buddhist nuns.
Dana – generosity, giving.
Sangha – the Buddhist community. One of the Three Jewels of Buddhism.

Amazing facts

Traditionally, monks and nuns own only their three robes, a bowl for their food, a razor for shaving, a needle and ball of thread, a water filter and a walking stick. They follow Buddha's lifestyle of detachment from material and worldly concerns.

Common misconceptions

Many Buddhists are vegetarian but it is not true that Buddhists do not eat meat. Some Tibetan Buddhists eat meat and if a Theravada monk or nun is offered meat as dana they will accept it if the animal has not been specifically killed for them. The emphasis for Buddhists is avoidance of intentional killing. The principle of Right Livelihood forbids a Buddhist from becoming a butcher or fisherman.

Teaching ideas

● Discuss with the children what makes a community – perhaps use the class as an example.
● Visit a Buddhist temple or community and talk to the members about the life and work of the sangha.
● Watch the section on the sangha in the Clear Vision DVD, *Buddhism for Key Stage 2* (see Resources, page 33).

The shrine and worship

Subject facts

Images of the Buddha

When Buddha was alive his followers would show respect for him by making offerings and sitting quietly in his presence. Quite a long time after his death, probably about 500 years or so, Buddhist monasteries included a shrine room with a rupa (Buddha image).

Nowadays, people can have shrines at home or in a more public place like a **vihara**, temple or **pagoda**. Buddha images, whilst representing the man who lived in India 2500 years ago, can vary according to the Buddhist country in question. A trip around the various temples in Bodh Gaya (where Buddha became enlightened) illustrates how the rupa are made in the image of the people who made them. In the Thai temple the golden image looks Thai, in the Chinese temple the image looks Chinese, and so on. In The Friends of the Western Buddhist Order Centre in Birmingham, the shrine room contains a large image that looks decidedly Western. Buddhists believe it is the teaching of Buddha that is important rather than his image, and it is a teaching for all people in all places.

Nevertheless, images of Buddha do share some characteristics. They often have a kind of lump on the top of the head. This is called the 'ushnisha' and symbolises wisdom and enlightenment. The rupa have long ear lobes to remind followers that those ears once wore the gold earrings of a prince who gave up worldly power. A 'spot' in the centre of the forehead of Buddha stands for the 'third eye' called the 'dhamma eye'. This is a traditional Indian symbol and can also be seen on Hindu **murtis**, for example the god Shiva (see pages 71–2). Buddha's face always displays great calm and compassion and he is very often sitting in a lotus position. This position gives the body great stability and people who regularly meditate in this position can sit for a long time. Buddha will be sitting on a lotus plant, a symbol of enlightenment (see pages 12–13). The image also includes a simple robe. This is to show that Buddha lived a very simple life with few possessions.

A very important part of the Buddha image is the position of the hands, called a *mudra* (symbolic gesture). There are many different mudras in Buddhist iconography and they all display different spiritual ideas. These include, amongst others, fearlessness, earth-touching and meditation (see Figure 2).

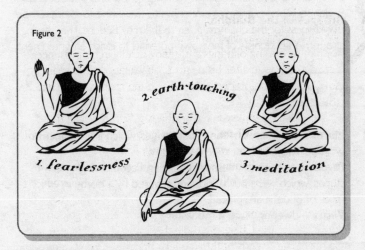

Figure 2

1. fearlessness

2. earth-touching

3. meditation

Other Buddhist images

Traditionally all Buddhist shrines will include the rupa. In Mahayana shrines there may also be other images of bodhisattvas (see page 9).

In all forms of Buddhism, candles, flowers and incense are offered to the shrine. The light reminds Buddhists of the wisdom of Buddha, which lights up the darkness of human confusion and ignorance. The flowers stand for impermanence – they are beautiful things but after a short while they wither and die. The incense reminds Buddhists of the importance of loving attitudes, which result in good actions – just as the scent of the incense spreads throughout a building, so good actions reverberate throughout the world. There are also seven offering bowls that symbolise the seven things traditionally offered in India to an honoured guest: water for washing, water to drink, flowers to garland the visitor, incense, light, perfume and food. Buddhists offer these to Buddha as an honoured guest.

Usually a member of a Buddhist community will, on entering the shrine room where the Buddha image is kept, make an offering to the image. This often involves the lighting of incense sticks and prostration before the image.

Buddhism

Why you need to know these facts

Ritual and devotion to Buddha play an important part in Buddhist practice. The focus of Buddhist worship is not God but Buddha. Buddhists worship and make offerings to the shrine to express their thankfulness for the dhamma given to them by Buddha. The offerings also remind Buddhists of their own potential to reach enlightenment.

Vocabulary

Murtis – the images of the Hindu deities, which are the focus of worship. The word 'murti' means 'form'.

Pagoda – a shrine or memorial building. Pagodas originate with stupas, which were burial mounds covered by a dome in which relics of Buddha are placed.

Vihara – dwelling place; a monastery.

Common misconceptions

Although the focus of worship is Buddha, Buddhists do not worship Buddha. The image reminds Buddhists of the qualities of enlightenment. In many respects the image is an inspiration for the individual to continue growing towards enlightenment. Worship encourages positive attitudes like determination, joy and inspiration which help in the practice of the dhamma.

Teaching ideas

● Make a Buddhist shrine in the classroom; artefacts are available from the Clear Vision Trust: **www.clear-vision.org**.
● Visit a Buddhist temple and ask if some of the children can be shown how a Buddhist makes offerings to the Buddha image.

● Discuss the different hand gestures the children know. Get them to illustrate them and their meanings. Discuss the positive and negative things people can do with their hands.

Buddhist Festivals

Subject facts

Buddhist festivals are based on the lunar calendar of particular countries and their dates and meanings vary according to the cultural origins of the Buddhist group concerned. This can make studying Buddhist festivals complicated indeed.

The most important festivals remember the birth, life, death and teachings of Buddha. The biggest festival is Wesak (Sri Lankan Buddhism) or Vaisakha Puja (Theravada Buddhism) or Buddha Day (Western Buddhism). It celebrates the birth, enlightenment and Parinibbana (passing away) of Buddha and takes place on full moon day in May. Mahayana Buddhists have three separate days for these three aspects, and celebrate the enlightenment on Bodhi Day in December.

Individual Buddhist countries celebrate a great variety of festivals but most Buddhist festivals include a time when the lay people come to the temple or vihara and join in with the monks' activities. They bring offerings and food for the monks. There is chanting of scriptures, teaching and meditation. Festivals are times for renewing commitments, especially to the Five Precepts. Some lay members take on extra precepts such as fasting for a short period.

Some Buddhist festivals celebrated in Britain are:
● **Kathina Day** (October, Theravada tradition). Lay members offer new robes to the monks.
● **Hanamatsuri** (April, Mahayana tradition). A flower festival remembering Buddha's birth in the garden at Lumbini. An infant Buddha image is bathed and placed in a floral shrine.
● **Parinibbana**, the Mahayana celebration in February of the passing away of Buddha. This day is called Nirvana Day by Pure Land Buddhists.

Buddhism

Why you need to know these facts

Buddhist festivals vary enormously depending on the country and culture concerned. Nevertheless celebration, particularly of the birth, life, death and teachings of Buddha, is important for Buddhists and is an important theme for RE.

Teaching ideas

- Get the children to write and illustrate a guide for non-Buddhists about Wesak or Buddha Day. Guidebooks about Buddha's birth and teachings could be produced.
- Contact a local Buddhist centre and ask if you can visit during a festival.
- Get the children to think about what commitments they might renew or make when it is their birthday.

Resources

Buddhist stories can be obtained from the Birmingham Buddhist Centre, 11 Park Road, Birmingham B13 8AB (0121 449 5279) or other Buddhist centres.

Artefacts suppliers
Religion in Evidence, TTS Group Ltd, Park Lane Business Park, Kirkby-in-Ashfield, Nottinghamshire NG17 9GU, 0800 318 686. www.tts-group.co.uk
Articles of Faith, Resource House, Kay Street, Bury BL9 6BU, 0161 763 6232, **www.articlesoffaith.co.uk**

TV programmes
Channel 4 *Animated World Faiths* series for ages 7–11.
Channel 4 *Stop, Look, Listen*, 'Water, Moon, Candle, Tree and Sword'. Suitable for Key Stage 1 children.
The Monkey King and Other Tales – a video and book package available from Clear Vision, 16/20 Turner Street, Manchester M4 1DZ, 0161 839 9579, **www.clear-vision.org**
Buddhism for Key Stage 2, also by Clear Vision.

Useful books
Religion in Focus: Buddhism by Geoff Teece (Franklin Watts, 2008).
Create and Display: Festivals by Claire Tinker (Scholastic, 2010).

Useful websites
www.bbc.co.uk/religion/religions/buddhism
www.chiddingstone.kent.sch.uk/homework/religion/buddhism.htm
www.firstschoolyears.com/re/buddhism/buddhism.htm
www.reonline.org.uk
http://retoday.org.uk

Chapter 2

Christianity

The Christian religion began about 2000 years ago with the life and work of Jesus of Nazareth. Jesus was a Jew and his earliest followers were also Jews. In one sense it is possible to say that Christianity began as a movement within Judaism. After Jesus' death and resurrection, these early followers believed Jesus to be the **Messiah**, or **Christ**, who was promised in the Jewish scriptures.

Christian tradition tells us that 50 days after the death of Jesus the **Holy Spirit** (understood to be the presence or power of God) came to those early followers during the Jewish festival of Shavuot. Christians now call this Pentecost and this time is now recognised as the beginning of the Christian Church. These events are recorded in the Bible in the Acts of the Apostles.

The development of the Christian Church has been a complex story. From very early times, the Church has had two distinct traditions called the Eastern and Western Church, the Western church centred upon Rome and the Eastern on Constantinople (now Istanbul). In 1054 there occurred what became known as the Great Schism. This revolved around a number of disagreements, including disagreements over the authority of the Pope who Western, or Roman Catholic, Christians believed to be the head of the church.

However, what ultimately caused the break was an argument about a clause in the Christian statement of belief called the **Nicene Creed** (325CE). By the 12th century, these differences resulted in two distinctive forms of Christianity: Eastern Orthodox and Roman Catholic.

It was the West that saw the next great division within the Christian Church. The tension between state and Church in the 16th century resulted in a split into Catholicism and Protestantism. The Protestant Churches often became national Churches and identified with the state, and as a consequence rejected the authority of the Pope in religious and spiritual matters.

In subsequent years, leading right up to the 21st century, both Catholic and Protestant traditions engaged in a worldwide mission to spread Christianity – there are now Christian communities on every continent on Earth. This has lead to the development of the Ecumenical Movement, with its aims and desire to fulfil the intention of Jesus that there should be unity within the Church.

There are an estimated 2.1 billion Christians in the world today. How then do we describe this huge and complex religious tradition? It is possible to group Christians under various ecclesiastical families such as Roman Catholic, Protestant, Orthodox, non-white indigenous (for example the United Church of Zambia), Anglican, Protestant sects (for example the Mormon Churches) and so on. However, while most Christians have a denominational identity, many feel a close affinity with Christians of other denominations who share the same or similar theological views. For example, standpoints such as **Fundamentalism**, **Traditionalism** or **Ecumenism** are very important for many Christians and often cross denominational boundaries.

Christianity is the largest and oldest religion in the UK. Despite reports of decreasing church attendance, some sources estimate that about 42 million people in the UK regard themselves as Christians and there are almost 50,000 registered Christian places of worship in England and Wales alone.

God and human nature

Subject facts

Basic Christian beliefs

Christians believe that all life comes from God and that everything belongs to him. They believe that he is good and provides for everyone on earth. And the most basic Christian belief is that there is only one God. This **monotheism** is affirmed at the beginning of the Ten Commandments and at the start of the Nicene Creed – the Christian statement of belief, written in 325CE.

Like many other traditions, Christians believe that God created the world. The account of the creation can be found in the Bible in Genesis 1–2 and expresses some key beliefs about the relationship between God and the world. Christians believe that the world depends on God, that all life is good and comes from God and that human beings have a special place in God's world. They also believe that humans have a responsibility to look after the world that God has created; they believe they are **stewards** of the world for God. Christians differ, however, in the way they interpret the creation stories in the Bible. Some see them as actual explanations of the way the world began. Others see them as myths – stories of poetic imagination that express truths about human experience and ideas about God.

Christians also believe that God is actively involved in the world he has created: he maintains its order; he guides its history; he controls its destiny. Perhaps the most important belief, however, is found in the idea that God reveals himself and his will to people. God, it is said, cannot be known and understood by human beings – he is too great, too holy and too powerful – but he has chosen to allow people to see something of his greatness and holiness and power. Those who have faith can see these things in the world around them, in its beauty, its order and its wonder. God has also revealed himself to people through his prophets, whom he has chosen. For example, he revealed himself to Abraham, to Moses, to Isaiah and to the other prophets of the Old Testament.

However, most importantly, Christians believe that God has revealed himself through Jesus who they believe was the Son of God. Most Christians refer to Jesus as God **incarnate**, which literally means 'the putting on of flesh'. In other words, for Christians, Jesus is God in human form.

The Holy Trinity

Christians refer to God in three ways: as Father, Son and Holy Spirit. As we have seen, God is the Father of Jesus Christ (the Son) and God's presence or power can be felt or experienced by Christians today in the form of the Holy Spirit. The first Christians wanted to avoid any idea that there was more than one God but they also wanted to make it clear at the same time that God, Jesus and the Holy Spirit were different. So they referred to one God in three persons. Christians call this the Holy **Trinity**. This is a complicated doctrine, and debates about its meaning have often divided the Christian community.

Children of God

Christians believe that all people, whether they are Christians or not, are children of God and consequently equal in the sight of God. Christians also believe that human beings are made 'in the image of God'. Christians understand this differently. For some it suggests that people have free will to act as they wish, and to choose between what is good and what is bad. It is this quality that distinguishes human beings from the animal kingdom, which relies on instinct.

However it can also suggest that God has given human beings special responsibility to act as his servants in exercising control over the world they live in, over all other living creatures and over their environment.

Some have interpreted the idea that humans are made in the image of God to suggest that, like God, they are immortal. Therefore the soul of every human being is part of God and never dies.

Humans and sin

A fundamental belief about God and human nature according to Christians is that this 'image of God' has been lost, at least in part. Genesis records how Adam and Eve were expelled from the Garden of Eden for disobeying God and eating the fruit from the Tree of Knowledge of good and evil. This story of human disobedience is believed by most Christians to be a myth that explains how human nature is imperfect, unsatisfactory or incomplete. For Christians, this means that all human beings have a tendency to turn away from God and to please themselves. This is called **sin**. It leads to doing wrong; it leads to humans putting themselves above or in the place of God and it leads to characteristics of the human ego such as selfishness and pride.

Some Christians continue to accept the traditional teaching of the Church that the disobedience of Adam and Eve has permanently tainted humans so that sin is passed on from generation to generation. Consequently all babies have this taint of original sin handed down from their parents. This can only be removed through the sacrament of baptism (see pages 50–1).

Other Christians, whilst they accept the spiritual truth of the story and believe that this inclination to turn away from God is very real, prefer to use the term 'fallenness'. They believe that human beings have fallen away from the image of God in which they were created. This fallenness explains the presence of evil and suffering in the world.

God's love

Finally, arguably the most important Christian belief is that God's nature is love. This is expressed many times in the history of Christian belief. For example, in the Bible St John writes:

> *God is love, and whoever lives in love lives in union with God, and God lives in union with him.*

> 1 John 4: 16

And God's greatest act of love was to send his only son, Jesus Christ, to save humanity from sin. As we have discussed, the disobedience of Adam and Eve caused a separation between humans and God. Christians believe that through sending Jesus to save humanity, the original relationship between God and humanity can be restored.

Why you need to know these facts

For Christians, belief in God is a way of responding to and interpreting the mystery of life and creation. Questions arising out of the human perception of the mystery of life are common to all people. Therefore, in terms of religious education, it is important to concentrate on the Christian ideas of God as creator and father of humankind. In this way it is possible to explore with children questions about creation and human responsibility towards the earth as well as questions about how humans should treat each other. These are rich themes for RE.

Vocabulary

Holy Spirit – the third aspect of God in the Holy Trinity. Active as a divine presence and power in the world and in dwelling in believers to make them like Christ and empower them to do God's will.

Incarnation – the doctrine that God took human form in Jesus Christ. It is also the belief that God in Christ is active in the Church and in the world.

Monotheism – belief in only one God.

Sin – an act of rebellion or disobedience against God. The human condition in need of transformation.

Stewardship – the belief that God has chosen humanity to be his servants and vice-regents with responsibility for the world.

Trinity – God in three persons: God the Father, God the Son (Jesus Christ) and God the Spirit (the Holy Spirit).

Sensitive issues

It was at the Council of Nicea in 325CE that the doctrine of the Trinity was formalised. Since then, some groups have rejected this. The Unitarians, some of whom regard themselves as Christians, reject the idea of God as three persons in one and, consequently, reject the idea of Jesus as divine. The Unitarians tend to be rejected by mainstream Christianity.

Amazing facts

The term 'Christianity' covers such a huge variety of beliefs and practices that it perhaps shouldn't be a surprise that there are people who call themselves Christians but don't believe in God; at least not a real God that exists separate from us, as described above. Anthony Freeman, a Christian priest, was dismissed from his living for writing a book called *God in Us*. This explained in a fairly accessible way the views of theologians like Don Cupitt and the Sea of Faith Group. Such views understand God as a metaphor for the highest human values. This is a view expressed by the 19th century German thinker Ludwig Feurbach. This view about God has come to be known as Christian Non-Realism.

Teaching ideas

● Look at passages in the Bible that describe God, for example Genesis 1: 26–31 and Psalm 8: 3–6, and discuss what can be learned from them about how Christians understand God.

● Read the Creation story in Genesis and discuss what it tells us about Christian views of God.

● Get the children to write poems that describe creation as they see it.

● Read *Dinosaurs and all that Rubbish*, by Michael Foreman (Puffin Books, 1993). Compare the message of this book with the Genesis story.

● Read the 'Parable of the Good Samaritan'. What does this story tell us about God's intentions for human relationships?

● Look at Biblical stories that express the belief that God's will ultimately triumphs over evil, such as David and Goliath, Joseph and his brothers, the resurrection of Jesus, the conversion of St Paul.

Jesus

Subject facts

Perhaps the one belief that most unites all Christians is belief in Jesus, yet Christians hold many complex beliefs about him. Traditionally, beliefs about Jesus have been studied under three headings: the Jesus of history, the Christ of faith and the Jesus of experience.

The Jesus of history

Jesus of Nazareth lived nearly 2000 years ago in the country we now call Israel. The Bible records that Jesus was born in Bethlehem and was killed when he was about 30 years old. He lived and taught around the area known as Galilee. His teachings proclaimed the coming of the Kingdom of God. There was a strong belief among the Jewish people at the time that a Messiah would come to them and bring forth a new age of peace and prosperity and free the Jewish people from their enemies, particularly the Romans. The early followers of Jesus believed Jesus to be the Messiah.

In the Jewish tradition at the time, people were immersed in water after they were initiated into the religion. Following this example, Jesus was baptised by John the Baptist to signify the start of his ministry. Some time after Jesus' death, baptism became part of the initiation into the Christian Church. Jesus chose 12 men to be his followers, or disciples, and they accompanied him on his journeys. Jesus' message was quite revolutionary at the time. He taught that all people could enter the Kingdom of God – in other words, all humans were equal in the sight of God. Such teachings got him into trouble with the Jewish authorities and ultimately contributed to his death.

The life and teachings of Jesus are recorded in the Bible in the four **Gospels** (good news). They were written after the death of Jesus and are now referred to as the Gospels of Matthew, Mark, Luke and John.

Attempts to reconstruct an accurate and detailed account of Jesus' life have always been controversial and present many challenges. Many Christians believe that every story in the Gospels is accurate, biographical material. Other Christians feel that it is important to subject the Gospels to historical and literary critical examination in order to make it relevant for Christians living in the world today.

Nevertheless, the story of the life of Jesus is central for all Christians. It is a central defining characteristic of being a Christian. The regular retelling of this story provides the basis for Christian worship and it is the central focus of all devotions and study. From it Christians draw their sense of identity and in the example of Jesus they find the inspiration and motivation to live a Christian lifestyle. The calendar of Christian festivals is structured around the life of Jesus. Remembering and celebrating his life is an essential part of most Christians' faith.

It is possible to group stories about Jesus under headings related to different stages in his life. A knowledge of these is essential for understanding the Christian religious tradition. These stories include his:

Birth: Joseph and Mary and the move to Bethlehem.
            Birth of Jesus in a stable.
            Visits of the shepherds and wise men.
            Herod and the escape to Egypt.

Boyhood: Visit of Mary, Joseph and Jesus to the temple
            in Jerusalem.

Ministry: Baptism by John the Baptist.
            Temptations in the wilderness.
            Calling of 12 disciples.
            Preaching and teaching.
            Healing and other miracle stories.

Passion: Clashes with Jewish and Roman authorities.
            Entry into Jerusalem on a donkey.
            Washing of disciples' feet.
            Celebration of the Lord's Supper.
            Betrayal, arrest and trial.
            Crucifixion.
            Resurrection.
            Appearances after his resurrection.
            Ascension into Heaven.

The Christ of faith

As well as his life story, theological beliefs about Jesus have always been important for Christians. Many of these ideas are conveyed through the stories and celebrations of his life, but there is also a variety of theological ideas connected with him. A variety of titles are given to Jesus. Five of the most common are **Lord**, Saviour, Son of God, Messiah and Christ. These titles all relate in some way to the key Christian belief that Jesus was God incarnate – a central tenet of the faith of most Christians.

In general terms, Jesus, as the *Christ*, is believed to be the Son of God who through his life, teaching, death and resurrection, **atones** for the sin of humankind and brings them back into a right relationship with God. For many, the life of Jesus represents a new covenant between God and the whole of humanity.

Christ is for all people in all times and all places. This is illustrated perfectly in the Gospels by Jesus' dealings with non-Jews (gentiles) and women. Jesus' treatment of these groups is revolutionary for the time and illustrates perfectly the Christian belief that all people are the children of God.

The term *Messiah* referred to one who would deliver the Jewish people from their enemies. For the early Christians, who were Jews, Jesus was that figure. The more popular term *Christ* comes from a Greek word equivalent to the Hebrew word Messiah.

The Jesus of experience

For many Christians, Jesus is not only the most important figure in history, nor is he just the incarnation of their religious beliefs and practice. He is a living person who shares in their personal experience and with whom they have a personal relationship.

When Christians say they experience Jesus it means that they meet and are constantly aware of his presence and that he provides the inspiration for their lives. Christians' experience of Jesus might include: a kind of mystical state of consciousness during which they feel that they are directly in touch with the living Christ; powerful experiences of a nearness of Christ, making urgent and inescapable demands on the person concerned; or a more subtle awareness of the presence of Christ, who befriends, supports and guides the person in all aspects of his or her life. For many Christians, belief in Jesus as a living person lies at the heart of Christian spirituality.

Why you need to know these facts

Belief in Jesus is the most important part of being a Christian. In terms of religious education, the life and teachings of Jesus present a marvellous opportunity for children to understand Jesus as a model for humankind. His life and teachings are a direct challenge to many contemporary ideas about human nature and behaviour. His teachings in relation to possessions, treatment of enemies, forgiveness, love and peace are ideal ways for children to begin to develop a critical view of the world in which they live.

Vocabulary

Atonement – reconciliation between God and humanity; restoring the relationship broken by sin. Sinners are therefore made 'at one' with God through the life, death and resurrection of Jesus.

Christ – the 'anointed one'; the Messiah; one of the titles given to Jesus by his followers.

Gospel – 'good news' of salvation in Jesus Christ; the part of the Bible that is an account of Jesus' life and work.

Lord – title used for Jesus to express his divine lordship over people, time and space.

Messiah – used in the Jewish tradition to refer to the expected leader who will bring the Jewish people to salvation. Jesus' followers used this title to refer to him.

Sensitive issues

Some Christian groups, like the Quakers, may not believe that Jesus was God incarnate, or at least not exclusively so. However most Christians believe that Jesus was God in human form. Whether this belief is exclusivist (that is, all other views of God are false) is not always certain but the incarnation is the most important aspect of Christian belief for many, and hence needs to be dealt with in a knowledgeable and sensitive way.

Amazing facts

Jehovah's witnesses reject Jesus as a person of the divine Trinity but believe that he was originally the Archangel Gabriel who was one of the two sons of Jehovah (God), the other son being Satan.

Teaching ideas

● Write a class biography of the life of Jesus. Compile it into an illustrated class book.
● Collect a variety of pictures of Jesus and get children to reflect on what he might have looked like: *Does it matter? Why do Christians think Jesus is special?*
● Set up a guided fantasy where Jesus comes back to earth and visits your local town: *What would he do? What might change?* Get children to write about this.
● Look at Jesus' teachings that challenge some of today's consumer values, for example, 'The Sermon on the Mount', 'The Rich Young Ruler', 'Dives and Lazarus'.

The Church and worship

Subject facts

Church

The word Church is used in three ways by Christians. Essentially it is a concept that is often referred to as the 'body of Christ'. This refers to all Christians, sometimes called the 'totality of believers' or the 'communion of saints', who are, or should be, a unity that physically continues the work of Christ after his resurrection. The day of Pentecost, when the Holy Spirit 'came down' to the first apostles of Jesus, is traditionally regarded as the beginning of the Christian Church.

Secondly, the word Church is also used to describe the different denominations of the Church that can be found around the world today. Finally, it is used to describe each local community and also the building that the community uses for worship.

The idea of the Church being the 'body of Christ' is the most important use of the term for Christians. The Christian creeds state that the Church is 'one, holy, catholic and apostolic'. The term 'one' denotes the Christian belief that Christ intended there be only one Church and that whilst diversity may be appropriate, division is not. The term 'holy' reflects the idea of the Christian community being in some way 'chosen' to be the physical presence of Christ in the world. The term 'catholic' means universal (rather than referring to the denomination of that name); it implies that the Church is worldwide and continuous through history. The term 'apostolic' reflects the belief of Christians that their faith and practice is in direct line with the first followers of Jesus, the Apostles. This belief is expressed in different ways. In some churches, like the Roman Catholic Church, it is reflected in the authority of the Pope and the Bishops, who represent an unbroken line of descendants, the **Apostolic Succession**. In other churches, the term refers more to the continuation of the teaching of Christ.

Worship

Worship in different churches takes many forms. Most include such activities as praying, reading of the Bible, preaching, singing hymns and giving money. However, different churches have quite different ways of worshipping. Some examples are:

● *The Orthodox Church.* These, like many churches, are usually built in the shape of a cross. Orthodox Churches are often highly decorated with frescos and **icons**, which adorn the whole interior of the building. These icons – rich pictures of the Trinity or saints – are aids to the worshippers, helping them to concentrate on their beliefs about God, Jesus and the Church. The main service is Divine **Liturgy**, which takes place on a Sunday and lasts for about three hours. Such services are highly ritualistic and colourful. They include the use of incense, the processing of the Bible and the kissing of icons. The worshippers stand for the whole service, which is divided into two sections: the 'liturgy of the word' and the 'liturgy of the sacrament'.

● *The Roman Catholic Church.* The main act of worship for Roman Catholics is **Mass**. This is a service led by a priest and includes Holy Communion (see pages 51–3). The building, shaped like a cross, usually contains statues, paintings and other visual items, especially of the Virgin Mary. Worshippers sit on seats or pews and face the altar. The service lasts for about an hour and includes singing of hymns, readings from the Bible, listening to a sermon and taking bread and wine. The Mass follows a liturgy contained in a book called a **Missal**. It takes place several times on a Sunday and during the week; in large churches Mass is held every day.

● *The Society of Friends (Quakers)*. Members of the Society worship in a building called a 'meeting house'. The buildings are usually plain and contain a meeting room where concentric circles of chairs are placed around a central table. Sometimes this table contains a focus for worship, such as a vase of flowers. The essence of the 'meeting' is that the worshippers sit in silence and await the inspiration of the 'spirit'. Often there are long periods of silence punctuated by a member, who has been 'moved' to speak, rising to his or her feet. The member might then give a personal testimony, or read from the Bible or from the Quaker pamphlet, 'Notes and Queries'. Anyone is allowed to speak and the meeting lasts for about one hour.

● *The Church of God of Prophecy*. This is just one of the many **Pentecostal** and/or **Evangelical churches** led by members of the black community found in large cities in Britain today. The focus here is on the preaching of the 'Word of God' and great emphasis is placed on readings from the Bible and the sermon, which can last for anything up to an hour. Joyful singing and the playing of modern instruments, like electric guitars, drums and electric pianos, accompany these elements. The churches usually have choirs who lead the singing. Members often clap when singing and utter shouts of praise, such as 'Hallelujah'. People often pray out loud or offer personal testimonies about their faith. Services often end with a call for people to kneel at a rail at the front of the church to receive the laying on of hands – a leader in the church physically lays his or her hands on the person's head as an act of healing spiritual problems by the Holy Spirit.

The cross
The cross is a major Christian symbol, used as a focus for Christian worship, that represents the crucifixion and resurrection of Jesus – the most important event for Christians. There are very many types of crosses, too innumerable to go into here.

A plain, wooden cross is often found in Protestant Churches. This cross emphasises the resurrection of Jesus – the cross is empty. In Roman Catholic Churches, among others, the crucifix, a cross with the figure of Jesus crucified, is more common and emphasises the suffering of Jesus for the sins of the world.

Why you need to know these facts

Most people experience the desire to belong to a group. At this level, the Christian Church offers individuals a deep sense of belonging, which gives Christians an identity that extends beyond the boundaries of family, country or race. The Church has enabled individual Christians to express themselves creatively, whether in terms of art or their mission in carrying out God's will. In terms of RE for primary children, the aspects of belonging and identity provide a rich resource for teaching.

Vocabulary

Apostolic Succession – the historical link between the Church and the first followers of Jesus.

Evangelical Church – group or church placing particular emphasis on the Gospel and the scriptures as the sole authority in all matters of faith and conduct.

Icons – paintings or mosaics of Jesus Christ, the Virgin Mary, saints or Church feasts. Used as an aid to worship and devotion, usually in the Orthodox tradition.

Liturgy – a service of worship, for example Eucharist or Evensong, that follows prescribed rituals. Used in the Orthodox Church for Eucharist.

Mass – term used by Roman Catholics and others for the Eucharist.

Missal – the book containing words and ceremonial directions for saying Mass.

Pentecostal Church – the branch of the Church that emphasises certain gifts that were given to the first believers on the Day of Pentecost (for example, to heal the sick and speak in tongues).

Sensitive issues

It is very easy to give the impression that Christianity is, essentially, a white, English-speaking, Western religion. When using examples of worship, for instance, try to include a variety that accurately reflects the great cultural diversity of Christianity.

Amazing facts

According to Christian sources, there are over 20,000 distinct denominations of the Christian Church.

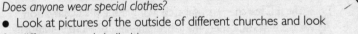

Teaching ideas

● Discuss with the children different groups to which they belong: *Is there a special building? Do you do special things there? Does anyone wear special clothes?*
● Look at pictures of the outside of different churches and look for differences and similarities.
● Visit a variety of churches: get children to spot distinctive features, ask the priest or minister to explain about the worship. Ask the children to look for things that remind them of God or make them think of him.
● Get the children to collect examples of different Christian symbols found in churches and find out what they mean.
● Discuss the feelings of belonging that people have when they meet regularly with other people who share their own ideas and interests.
● Find out about the other work of a local church, such as social activities, caring mission and so on.

The sacraments

A sacrament is an outward sign of an inward blessing. Traditionally, there are seven sacraments for Christians and they are an important means for helping Christians to develop spiritually and to live a life as exemplified by Jesus. Nowadays, most Christians believe that baptism and Holy Communion are the most important sacraments, and these are the two that are emphasised in Protestant Churches. The other five sacraments – Confirmation, Marriage, Penance, Anointing the sick and Ordination – have a greater emphasis in the Roman Catholic and Orthodox traditions.

Baptism

Baptism is a major sacrament for most Christians. It remembers Jesus' baptism by John the Baptist and it is, for many, the way of celebrating and ritualising their commitment to live a life like Jesus and their joining the Christian Church. Some receive this sacrament when very young, whilst others are baptised later in life when they feel able to make a personal commitment to live life as a Christian. Baptism is not just an initiation ceremony, however. It is for many a vital step along the path to **salvation**. As we have already seen, the Christian view of Human Nature is that human beings have fallen away from God's intentions for them. It is through baptism that a Christian makes a commitment to turn away from sin and towards God.

When a person is baptised, a leader in the church sprinkles water on the head of the person being baptised, or dips or completely immerses his or her whole body in water. The church leader remembers the Trinity saying, 'I baptise you in the Name of the Father, the Son and the Holy Spirit.' When this is done, the original sin of the person being baptised is 'washed away' so enabling him or her to lead a new life in Christ. The person is asked if they are prepared to live life as a Christian. When a baby is baptised, the parents and godparents (people chosen by the family to play a particular role in the child's spiritual life) make these promises for the child.

There are many powerful symbolic aspects of baptism. The church leader makes the sign of the cross on the person's forehead. The person being baptised might wear white to symbolise purity. He or she is given a lighted candle to symbolise Jesus Christ who brought light to the world. This baptismal candle is lit in the Church from the **Paschal candle**. On Easter Day, when Christians celebrate the resurrection of Jesus, the Paschal candle is dipped three times in the **font** in many churches. This ritual makes a link between the resurrection of Jesus and the giving of light to the newly baptised. It signifies the baptised person's intention to lead a 'new' life as a follower of Christ.

The symbolic use of water for baptisms goes back to Jesus' baptism by John in the River Jordan. The word itself comes from the Greek word *baptizo* which means 'to dip'. As water is used for washing, the water in the baptism service symbolises the person's sins being washed away and the person receiving God's forgiveness. As water refreshes, the water in the ceremony also reflects the belief that baptism brings joy and happiness to the person. As water is essential for life, water in the ceremony reflects the belief that a relationship with God is essential for a person to live the best possible life. Those Christians who baptise by total immersion believe that by going fully under the water the person symbolically dies as the old self and rises up out of the water to be 'born again' into the Christian life.

Holy Communion

For most Christians, the sacrament of Holy Communion is the most important part of their worship of God. For many Christians, it is the clearest expression of Christian belief and the chief means for receiving the gifts of the Holy Spirit (see pages 36–7). The life of most Christian communities revolves around this sacrament. At Holy Communion, Christians remember Jesus' act during his last supper with his disciples, the night before his crucifixion, when he broke bread and identified it with his body and drank wine and identified it with his blood. This is so that all his followers would remember him. In services today, the priest or minister consecrates bread and wine by saying a special prayer called the Eucharist Prayer. The bread and wine are then distributed among the congregation.

Within the Christian Church a variety of names are used for this sacrament:

● *The Lord's Supper.* This recalls the story of the Bible about the last meal that Jesus had with his followers. It was during this supper that this sacrament, using bread and wine, was begun by Jesus.

● *The Eucharist.* Eucharist comes from a Greek word, *eucharistia*, meaning 'thanksgiving'. Therefore the Eucharist refers to a thankfulness that Christians have for what they believe Christ did for them through his life, death and resurrection.

● *Holy Communion.* Two things are stressed when this name is used. One is the idea that this is a sacred and holy ceremony because it was begun by Christ himself. The other is the idea that Christians meet together and with God in a special way during this sacrament. They have communion with God and with each other.

● *Mass.* Roman Catholics use this name for their regular act of worship, in which Holy Communion is the central ritual. This is why the word Mass is often thought of as another name for Holy Communion. The name comes from a Latin word *missa*, meaning 'sent'. At the end of worship, the congregation are dismissed – they are sent out to live their lives as Christians.

Churches have different rules about who may share in this sacrament. In some churches, all baptised people, however young, may receive the bread and wine; in others, only baptised people who have received special preparation and teaching may take part; sometimes taking communion is restricted to adult members of the church who have been confirmed; in other churches anybody who attends the service may join in.

For communion, most Churches use small, thin wafers of bread, specially made for this sacrament. Others may use ordinary bread from a shop. Some serve the wine in one goblet or **chalice**; all those sharing in the sacrament drink from this cup. Others, usually Non-Conformist Churches, such as Methodist and Baptist Churches, serve the wine in individual cups. Christian groups like the Methodists use non-alcoholic wine in this sacrament because they believe that alcohol is unhealthy or socially dangerous.

Some Christians see the bread and the wine as sacred or holy. These elements must therefore be treated with great care and reverence, for example a tray or cloth may be held under the communicant's chin to prevent any crumb or drop of wine falling to the floor. After the service, any remaining bread or wine will be consumed by the priest or kept in a special container, which looks like a chalice with a lid on it. It is called a 'ciborium' and is kept in a safe known as a 'tabernacle'. There is a light over this tabernacle, which is always kept alight to symbolise the presence of God.

Within the Church there are different understandings of the meaning of these elements. Roman Catholics believe that the Real Presence of Christ is in the wafer of bread because it has been consecrated. For many Catholics the bread and wine become Christ's body and blood, even though their outward appearances do not change. This is called Transubstantiation. Others interpret the elements as symbols and believe that Christ is present in a spiritual way and the bread and wine are reminders of the Last Supper. For Christians who hold this view sharing in this sacrament is the best way of becoming aware of Christ's presence and receiving his blessing. Nevertheless, most Christians believe that Christ is present in this sacrament in a special way that is mysterious. In Roman Catholic and **Anglican** services this mystery is expressed in the Eucharistic Prayer with the words, 'Let us proclaim the mystery of faith. Christ has died. Christ is risen. Christ will come again.'

Why you need to know these facts

The Christian sacraments link clearly to a general human experience of making commitments through outward or symbolic expression. Learning about the sacraments can be likened to examples from the children's own experiences of such outward signs, for example wearing badges or uniforms, flying flags, shaking hands.

Vocabulary

Anglican – Churches in full communion with the see of Canterbury. Their origins and traditions are linked to the Church of England.

Chalice – goblet for holding the communion wine.

Font – receptacle to hold water used in baptism.

Paschal candle – a large, special candle associated with Easter. In many Orthodox, Roman Catholic and Anglican churches, a fire is lit on Easter Eve and a new Paschal candle is lit from this fire. The candle is carried through the church, representing the light of Christ who, by his resurrection, conquered the powers of darkness and death.

Sacrament – an outward sign of an inward blessing. There are seven sacraments; the two most important are baptism and Eucharist.

Salvation – the process of being saved by Christ. Christians view the present human condition as being distorted and can only be transformed by the saving power of Jesus.

Common misconceptions

It would be a mistake to think that all Christian groups are sacramental. Groups like the Quakers and the Salvation Army may not keep any of the sacraments because they do not want to restrict God's grace and forgiveness to these rituals. For them, perhaps, the whole of life itself is a sacrament.

Teaching ideas

● Visit a church to look at the font and talk to the vicar or priest about infant baptism.

● Read about the baptism of Jesus by John in Matthew 3: 13–17.

● Read Mark 10: 13–16 about Jesus blessing young children. Talk about the idea that God loves all people including very young babies and that baptism is an expression of this.

● Show children artefacts connected with baptism or Holy Communion; get them to draw and label them, to illustrate their meaning.

● Get children to list what they think are the most important things in life and compare their ideas with the values expressed in Holy Communion.

Festivals (the church year)

Subject facts

Christians celebrate three major festivals: Christmas, Easter and Pentecost. Christmas and Easter celebrate parts of the story of Jesus – Christmas remembers his birth, while Easter focuses on his death and resurrection. Pentecost celebrates the birth of the Christian Church.

Christmas

The festival of Christmas is based on the stories of the birth of Jesus found in the Gospels. Most Christians celebrate Christmas on 25 December. The Eastern Orthodox Church celebrates Christmas on 7 January. For all Christians, Christmas is a time of celebrating Christ's birth by attending services in church, whether they be services of readings from the Bible and carols or the special Eucharist service of Midnight Mass held on Christmas Eve.

At Christmas, Christians express some of their most important beliefs about Jesus, four of which are:

● *Jesus is the Son of God.* The stories of the virgin birth, the angels, the shepherds and the wise men are different ways of expressing the central Christian belief (for most Christians) that Jesus is the Son of God. It is this belief that is the great unifying factor for Christians making them different from all other religious people.

● *Jesus is God incarnate.* 'Incarnation' is the doctrine that God took human form. At Christmas, Christians celebrate their belief that God came and lived on earth in the form of Jesus Christ.

● *Jesus is the fullest revelation of God.* Most Christians believe that God has made himself known to people in many ways. However they also believe that, as the Son of God, Jesus Christ is the best revelation of God that the world has ever received. All other ideas about God and about how people should live are inferior to those found in Jesus Christ.

● *Jesus is the centre of history.* Many hundreds of years after Jesus, Christians decided to begin numbering the years from the date of his birth. Countries which have been influenced by the Christian religion for a long time divide history into AD (*Anno Domini,* 'in the year of the Lord') and BC (Before Christ). This expresses the Christian belief that the birth of Jesus marks the centre of history.

Easter

Easter celebrates the resurrection of Jesus from the dead. It is held on a different date each year. In Britain, Easter Day may be on any Sunday between 22 March and 25 April.

The Easter festival celebrates the events of the last week in the life of Jesus, known as Holy Week. The week begins a week before Easter Sunday with Palm Sunday, when Jesus rode into Jerusalem on a donkey. Maundy Thursday remembers Jesus washing the disciples' feet and the Last Supper between Jesus and his disciples. Good Friday is an extremely solemn day that remembers Jesus' crucifixion, and this leads to the great joy of Easter Day and the celebration of his resurrection from the dead. As well as the beliefs expressed by Christians at Christmas, three other significant beliefs are celebrated at Easter:

● *Christians believe that God is love.* Jesus, as the Son of God, is full of love for all people. Two parts of the events of Holy Week point to this belief. On Palm Sunday, Jesus rides into Jerusalem on a donkey rather than a horse, to make the point that he came as a saviour expressing the love and peace of God, rather than the power of the world. Nailed to the cross on Good Friday, Jesus expresses his love as he prays to God, saying, 'Father, forgive them! They know not what they do.' Therefore Christians believe that Jesus came into the world to show that love and to inspire people to live together in love and peace.

● *Jesus is the Saviour of the world.* At Easter, Christians express their belief that Jesus sacrificed his life to show that love can destroy evil. In so doing he atoned for the sins of humanity and set them free from death. Christians declare a belief in the resurrection of Jesus. Through believing in him and by living a life close to God and following his example, Christians can also overcome the finality of death.

● *Jesus is alive and always present.* This most important Christian belief is expressed in the resurrection stories, which are celebrated on Easter Day. Christians believe, therefore, that Jesus can be worshipped and that his spirit can inspire and help people today.

Pentecost

Pentecost (from the Greek for 50) takes place 50 days after Easter Day. It celebrates the coming of the Holy Spirit to the followers of Jesus 50 days after his resurrection, as in the Bible in Acts of the Apostles. This event marks the beginning of a community of believers (the Church) who, by the power of the Holy Spirit, are able to carry on the work begun by Jesus. Pentecost is therefore the celebration of the birthday of the Christian Church. Three important beliefs are expressed in this festival:

● *The Trinity.* Christians believe that God exists in three forms: the Father, Son and Holy Spirit (see pages 36–7).

● *The Church as the body of Christ.* This is the belief that God's spirit lives in those who follow Jesus. Therefore Christians believe that all believers, together, are a new body which replaces that of the man, Jesus. This 'new body' is the Christian Church, the 'body of Christ'.

● *The fruits of the Spirit.* Many Christians believe that certain qualities of character are developed in their lives by the coming of the Holy Spirit. These are often referred to as the 'fruits of the Spirit' (see also page 51).

Why you need to know these facts

The desire to celebrate what we regard as important has always been a significant aspect of being human. For Christians it is important to celebrate the life of Jesus and theological ideas about the meaning of his life, as outlined on the previous pages. For the purposes of religious education, these three major festivals need to be studied if children are to gain an adequate understanding of Christianity.

Common misconceptions

It is probably due to increased secularisation and the dominance of the money culture that some people regard Christmas as the most important Christian festival. Whilst all three are highly significant, Easter and Pentecost are no less significant than Christmas. Indeed it is probably correct to say that Easter is the most important Christian festival in terms of its message for Christians about the truth of salvation realised by God in Christ at the Easter event.

Jehovah's Witnesses do not celebrate Christmas or Easter for a number of reasons. They believe that Jesus was born on or near 1 October, because this is when shepherds kept their flocks out of doors at night. Secondly, Jesus did not tell his followers to celebrate his birth but remember his death. Thirdly, Jehovah's Witnesses believe that both Christmas and Easter are based on the customs of 'ancient false religions'. Finally, the early Christians did not celebrate Christmas or Easter.

Teaching ideas

- Learn about, write about and draw the symbols connected with a variety of services held at Christmas designed to remember different aspects of the importance of Jesus, for example the Advent service, Midnight Mass or Christingle ceremony.
- Look at some Christmas carols and discuss what they tell us about what Christians believe about Jesus and why Christmas is important.
- Introduce Easter through the artefacts of Holy Communion and explain how Christians use the chalice, bread, wine and so on as ways of remembering the message of Easter.
- Read together the Easter story, concentrating on the Last Supper, Good Friday and Easter Sunday, and discuss what Christians remember about Jesus.
- Explore Easter symbols, for example the plain cross (emphasising the resurrection) and the crucifix (emphasising the suffering of Jesus for humanity).
- Explore links between Easter and baptism, for example

baptism as another way of remembering Jesus, and the baptismal candle being lit from the Paschal candle.

● Read the story of the first Pentecost, in Acts of the Apostles Chapter 2. Discuss what the church is and what the church as the 'body of Christ' might mean.

● Look at, illustrate and discuss the meanings of some symbols of Pentecost, for example fire and wind. Do the same for other symbols, such as the dove, breath or water.

● Watch a DVD of Pentecostal worship or visit a Pentecostal church and discuss how this reflects the emphasis on the holy spirit.

The Bible

Subject facts

The Christian Bible is often referred to as a 'library of books'. This term reflects the varied content of the Bible, which includes a great variety of writing. The Old Testament consists of the Law (Genesis to Deuteronomy), books of History (Joshua to Esther), books of Wisdom (Job to Song of Songs), and the Prophets (Isaiah to Malachi). The New Testament consists of history (the Gospels and the Acts of the Apostles), the letters (Romans to Jude) and the apocalyptic book called Revelations.

The word of God

For Christians, the Bible is the 'word of God'. How this term is understood amongst Christians depends to a great extent on how individual Christians and Churches understand the concept of authority. For most Christians, the Bible has authority for them because they believe it was written by people who were inspired by the Holy Spirit. Some Christians believe that the Bible has absolute authority because every word is the actual word of God. Therefore, for them, the Bible is the most important aspect of Christian belief because all other Christian beliefs can only be properly understood in terms of what the Bible says. The words of the Bible, therefore, do not need explaining for today because the message is timeless. God made the meaning plain to the people who wrote it down.

Other Christians believe that the Bible, whilst certainly inspired, is a human construct. The Bible was written in the ancient languages of Hebrew, Greek and Latin and the writers were addressing people who had a different world view from people today. For example, people today do not generally believe in the New Testament view of the universe, sometimes called the 'three-tier universe', of heaven above, earth in the middle and hell below. Consequently, statements like, 'Jesus ascended into heaven' need interpreting for today's world. Christians who hold these views about the Bible believe that only when the Bible is interpreted for today does it have real authority.

Interpreting the Bible

But who has the right to decide which interpretation of the Bible is correct? For some, like most Roman Catholics, only the Church in the person of the Bishops can decide on the Bible's meaning. This is because they are part of the Apostolic Succession of people who were sent out to preach the message of Jesus. For these Christians, the Bible belongs to the Church. According to this view, it was the Church that decided what should be included in the Bible, and it is through the Church that the message of the Bible has been handed down to people today. Other Christians, for example many **Protestants**, believe that the correct understanding of the Bible depends on the Holy Spirit. It is the Holy Spirit that inspires the believer to find meaning in the text.

Therefore, there has traditionally been these two views: one that says that the Church has authority over the Bible; and one that says it is the Bible, inspired by the Holy Spirit, that has authority over the Church. Such views are not held so rigidly today and, for many Christians, the Bible is the book that inspires their faith. It is a book that encourages Christians to believe in the truth of Jesus.

The use of the Bible

The importance of the Bible and the position of respect and authority it holds for most Christians can be seen in the many different practices that reflect these attitudes. In Orthodox Churches, the priest carries the Bible in a procession. The Church, often fairly dimly lit, is suddenly bathed in light when the priest brings out the Bible from behind the **iconostasis**. Members of Orthodox Churches may also kneel before the Bible or kiss it.

In most churches, special emphasis is placed on reading the Bible during services. The sermon is often an explanation of a passage from the Bible. In Orthodox, Roman Catholic and Anglican services, readings from the Bible form the 'liturgy of the word'. This leads up to the 'liturgy of the sacrament', at which point the people take communion. When the Gospel is read during the Eucharist service, people generally stand to show respect. This illustrates the belief amongst some Christians that some parts of the Bible are more important than others.

The Bible is the most important book for many Christians and Bible study is often a central feature of a Christian's life. In many countries the Bible has a significant role in public life. Its use in parliament and the courts of law reflect a belief in the values of the Bible, such as truth, justice and righteousness.

Why you need to know these facts

The Bible provides authoritative insights and guidance about how Christians should live their lives. As such, its content presents a challenge to contemporary society in terms of what is valuable and important in life. The theme of rules and guidance is a common one in RE, and teaching about the content of the Bible and how it is used in the Christian tradition will contribute effectively to such a theme.

Vocabulary

Iconostasis – a screen covered with icons used in Eastern Orthodox churches to separate the sanctuary (the part of the church that contains the altar, which is where the bread and wine are consecrated) from the nave (the main body of the church where the worshippers stand).

Protestant – the part of the Church that became distinct from the Roman Catholic and Orthodox traditions when their members professed or protested the centrality of the Bible and other beliefs. Protestants profess that the Bible under the guidance of the Holy Spirit is the ultimate authority for Christian teaching.

Sensitive issues

Because the Bible is such a commonplace object, it is easy to forget how precious it is to many Christians. Be careful, therefore, to show the Bible the respect that many Christians would want you to show.

Amazing facts

Bible societies, such as the British and Foreign Bible Society and the Wycliffe Bible Translators, work to translate the Bible so that it can be understood by everyone in the world. Despite this, there are still many people without a Bible that they can understand. Some scholars believe that there needs to be a new translation in every language every 30 years to meet the goal of worldwide access to a Bible.

Common misconceptions

People can be confused about where the Apocrypha fits into the Bible. Some copies of the Bible include the Apocrypha (hidden things), others do not. These writings are not considered as authoritative by many Christians, although Catholics do view the Old Testament Apocrypha as inspired and therefore as having authority.

Teaching ideas

● Explore examples of how the Bible is used in Christian worship (see pages 59–62). Make a chart to illustrate its use.
● Look at stories from the Bible that reflect some key Christian values, for example the story of the Good Samaritan and Jesus on the cross (compassion, forgiveness and love) and Exodus or Esther (justice and freedom).

Christian character

Living life as a Christian is about forming certain character traits. There are a number of these and they are referred to in the New Testament. All these characteristics can be found in the person of Jesus Christ, who remains the greatest model for Christians in how to live a life devoted to God. Jesus describes these values in the Beatitudes (Matthew 5: 3–10). Perhaps the clearest summary is found in St Paul's letter to the Galatians:

The Spirit produces love, joy, peace, patience, kindness, goodness, faithfulness, humility and self-control.
Galatians 5: 22–23

Love

Love is the most important character trait. The word has been reduced in meaning in contemporary society. The Greek word *agape* is usually used to describe the idea of Christian love. It is most comprehensively and beautifully described by St Paul in his letter to the Corinthians:

Love is patient and kind; it is not jealous or conceited or proud; love is not ill mannered or selfish or irritable; love does not keep a record of wrongs; love is not happy with evil; but is happy with the truth. Love never gives up; and its faith, hope and patience will never fail.
1 Corinthians 13: 4–7

Of course, for Christians, the real meaning of love is to be found in the example of Jesus, who sacrificed everything, including his life, for others, as noted in the Gospel of John:

My command is this: love each other as I have loved you. Greater love has no-one than this, that he lay down his life for his friends.
John 15: 12–13

According to Christian belief, this love should be shown to fellow Christians, the poor and needy, and even to enemies:

> *Love your enemies and pray for those who persecute you, so that you may become the sons of your Father in heaven.*
>
> Matthew 5: 44

When Jesus was asked what was the greatest commandment, he replied:

> *Love the Lord your God with all your heart, with all your soul, and with all your mind.*
>
> Mark 12: 29–30

Joy

For Christians, joy is more than just happiness. It is an attitude to God, the world and the rest of humanity. It is to be found in relationships with others. It is to be found in the beauty of God's creation. It helps Christians be strong when faced with difficulties; it is a reflection of great faith in God.

Peace

This is about promoting the well-being of others. It is about reconciliation and the bringing together of people. It is expressed ritually in Christian worship through the 'passing or sharing of the Peace' during the Eucharist and, in many churches, worshippers greet each other by saying 'Peace be with you'. The 'passing of the Peace' is a very important symbolic gesture of the power of Jesus to bring people together to forgive each other and find redemption.

Patience

Patience is about enduring hardship and not complaining. It requires a positive attitude to life because of the strength of a person's faith. It also means acting without anger or feelings of vengeance.

Faithfulness

Faithfulness means keeping to one's Christian principles no matter what the situation or the cost. This relates to many areas of life, for example in a Christian's promises of commitment in marriage.

Humility

Humility means that Christians should not think more highly of themselves than they should. It means that a person in a leadership role, for example, should remember that it is the duty of a Christian to serve other people. Humility excludes attitudes like arrogance and self-pride. A truly humble person is not weak but strong. A humble person does not jump to judgements about others. He or she is forgiving because nobody is perfect and all require the forgiveness of God.

Why you need to know these facts

It is important that children are given the opportunity to gain insight as to why people have a faith. Christian beliefs and practices are important in so far as they can be contextualised within an understanding of Christian spirituality. This is particularly the case if children have no prior contact with the Christian tradition.

Common misconceptions

While many Christians would hope to display the characteristics of gentleness and humility, it is not true, as some people (including the philosopher Neitzsche) think, that Christians are timid and weak. Christian spirituality includes a certain toughness of character and action. This is often expressed in terms of righteous indignation towards injustice and evil in the world. This is a defining characteristic of Jesus who, far from being meek and mild, often displayed righteous indignation. Examples include the overturning of the money lenders' tables (John 2: 13–17) and his criticisms of the hypocrisy of the religious leaders of his time (Matthew 23: 23–24).

Teaching ideas

- Discuss the characteristics of a good person.
- Read stories of Christians who have displayed Christian character traits, such as St Peter, St Stephen or St Francis.
- Produce a poster to illustrate the Christian idea of love.
- Write poems based on the 'furniture game' to enable children to describe each other's good qualities. For example: 'If Peter was a chair he would be…/ if he was a drink he would be…/ if he was an animal he would be…'
- Discuss the idea of forgiveness and help children explore their own attitudes towards this, maybe thinking about someone who has hurt them.
- Ask children to bring in pictures of people they love and who love them. Consider questions like: *Do we/should we only love those we know? How can we love people who are different? What about people who are unkind to us?*
- Read the story of *John Brown, Rose and the Midnight Cat* by Jenny Wagner (Puffin Books, 1980).

Resources

An excellent source of Bible stories are two volumes by Jack Priestley, called *Bible Stories for Classroom and Assembly* (Religious and Moral Education Press, 1993 and 1994).

Artefacts suppliers
Religion in Evidence (see page 33 for details).
Articles of Faith (see page 33 for details).

TV programmes (available on DVD)
BBC TV *Watch*
Channel 4 *Animated World Faiths* series for ages 7–11.
Channel 4 *Animated Bible Stories: The Life of Jesus* for ages 4–6.
Channel 4 *Stop, Look, Listen,* 'Water, Moon, Candle, Tree and Sword' for early years children.

Useful books

Religion in Focus: Christianity by Geoff Teece (Franklin Watts, 2008).
Create and Display: Festivals by Claire Tinker (Scholastic, 2010).

Useful websites

www.bbc.co.uk/schools/religion/christianity
www.reonline.org.uk
http://retoday.org.uk

Chapter 3

Hinduism

Of the six major religions, Hinduism is the one that teachers of Western origin often find most difficult to understand. People who live in the West have tended to view religions as 'systems of belief', often identified with a specific figure, a holy book, a number of key festivals related to the historical development of the faith and so on. Whilst many students of religion would say that this is an oversimplification of any religious tradition, in the case of Hinduism it really isn't like this at all!

'Hinduism' as a label for the religious traditions, beliefs and practices of the people of India only came into existence relatively recently. Historically, Hindus have referred to their religion as **Sanatan Dharma** (the eternal way). For many Hindus their religion goes beyond time and space: it is the eternal truth; it has no founder or teacher.

The word 'Hindu' is derived from the ancient civilisation based around the Indus River in the north of India, but Hinduism is a great mixture and mingling of traditions. It is often referred to as a 'way of life', and it is true to say that 'doing the right thing' is more important to Hindus than 'believing the right thing'. Hinduism is also a tradition within which it is very difficult to separate culture from religion. Westerners tend to separate the sacred from the secular – in India that is not really the case. Of course, there are some Hindus who take a more historical view of their belief and others who may refer to one Hindu as being more devout than another, but generally there is great tolerance within this religion, which manages to encompass a great myriad of different practices. However, there are basic ideas about life and ritual, God and the universe that are commonly accepted and are derived from the ancient scriptures. It is these ideas and rituals that we shall concentrate on in this chapter.

It is estimated that there are about 900 million Hindus in the world and up to half a million in the UK. The Hindu community in the UK is an ethnically diverse group. The majority originate from the Gujarat region; others are from the Punjab, Bengal and other northern and southern Indian states.

The Divine

Subject facts

Hindus appear to believe in many different gods. In truth they believe there is only one God, but they worship God in many forms.

Brahman

The oneness of God is to be found in Brahman. Brahman is the ultimate reality from which all created things come and to which all things ultimately go. Brahman is essentially a mystery – it is both beyond all things yet present in them all. It is beyond personification, it is beyond images of the deities and the idea of a personal God, and it is therefore, in its essence, indescribable. It is sometimes referred to as 'neither this nor that'. In one of the **Upanishads** it is written that 'the whole universe is Brahman'.

Hindus use the sacred symbol **aum** (see Figure 3), to stand for Brahman. Aum is the vibrating sound of the universe, which is made by the life-giving force of Brahman. It is often chanted as a **mantra** in meditation and worship and is found in all temples.

Figure 3

AUM

Brahman is represented by the Trimurti: the three deities of Brahma (the creator of the universe), Vishnu (the preserver of the universe) and Shiva (the destroyer and re-creator of the universe). The three deities are not separate in reality but aspects of the life-force of Brahman, creating, preserving and destroying and recreating the universe.

Murti

A murti (form) is an image of a god used as a focus for Hindu worship. Murtis can be elaborate marble forms, as seen in many Hindu temples, small plastic images as seen in homes, or images in colourful posters.

Each murti is richly decorated and full of symbolism. In each hand they hold objects that represent their divine powers. Murtis of Vishnu and Shiva are often purple or blue, representing their great spiritual power – the colour blue symbolises the sky, which is infinite, and so conveys the deity's infinite stature. Like human royalty, murti wear crowns and sit under canopies. An animal or bird also accompanies each murti. These creatures are known as the murti's 'vehicles' because they protect the murti and help it travel around the universe.

The murti of Brahma is usually pictured as having four heads facing the four directions of the compass. This symbolises God's creation of the whole universe. However, Brahma is not seen in temples as much as Vishnu and Shiva (see Figure 4 on the following page). This is because most Hindus are devotees of the latter two.

Vishnu

Vishnu's function is to maintain and preserve the harmony and order of the universe. All the symbols associated with Vishnu remind devotees that they need to keep and follow the moral law and live their lives through spiritual values to maintain the order of the universe. Vishnu is usually seen either lying on a cobra or with the cobra behind his head; the cobra symbolises cosmic time and energy. Vishnu is normally shown as blue, symbolising his infinite spiritual power. In three of his four hands are a conch shell (representing the music of the universe calling all people to live a pure, spiritual life), a discus or chakra (representing his power to maintain order) and a mace

Figure 4

Brahma   *Vishnu*   *Shiva*

from evil). He also holds, and is standing in, a lotus flower; this is a traditional Indian symbol of purity and enlightenment. Vishnu's vehicle is a huge bird called Garuda. Garuda is a great symbol of power and strength.

Because Vishnu is the preserver of the universe, Hindus believe that he appears on earth in a form known as an **avatar** (one who descends). An avatar represents the power of God to take any form, human or animal, in order that righteousness may be restored on Earth. There are nine avatars of Vishnu and the most important of these are Krishna and Rama.

Shiva

Shiva is seen in three different forms. As Shiva Nataraj or 'lord of the dance', he is seen dancing the world into existence within a cosmic circle of fire. He is standing on the demon of ignorance. For Hindus, avidya (meaning blindness or ignorance of spiritual truths) is the greatest obstacle to a spiritual fulfilment.

In another form, Shiva is depicted as a meditating **yogi** with the Himalayan mountains in the background. This symbolises his great purity of concentration in not being distracted by worldly things. He has matted hair, which caught the River Ganges as it flowed from heaven onto Earth; a cobra around his neck symbolises that he is beyond death; a tiger skin over his shoulder represents the need to overcome ignorance and pride; and he carries a trident, the symbol of a holy man who has withdrawn from the pleasures of a worldly life.

The third aspect of Shiva is the **lingum**. This symbolizes Shiva's creative and regenerating powers. It is a round stone pillar representing the linga (male reproductive organ) set in a circular stone representing the yoni (female reproductive organ). It is this form of Shiva to which worship is offered in temples.

Shakti

A very important form of God in Hinduism is that of the goddess which represents **shakti** (divine power). Shakti gives the universe energy and life. Shakti as the goddess takes a variety of forms, on her own or as a consort of the male gods mentioned above.

As a consort of Shiva she is Parvati or Uma and represents the gentle side of her nature, as a loving wife. As a consort to Vishnu she is Lakshmi, goddess of wealth, prosperity and good fortune. As consort to Brahma she is Saraswati, goddess of spiritual knowledge of the nature of Brahman. She holds the sacred scriptures and plays a vina (an Indian musical instrument like a small sitar) which represents the sound of aum.

On her own the goddess takes the form of Durga or Kali. Both are powerful figures. Durga is usually shown riding a tiger, illustrating her power in controlling such an animal with great strength. She carries weapons to kill the demon buffalo, which represents ignorance. As Kali, the goddess is in her most terrifying form. Shown dark or black in colour she has many heads with a tongue dripping blood. She wears a garland of skulls and holds a severed head in her hand. These symbols represent her great power in destroying evil.

Why you need to know these facts

Because Hindu ideas of God are complex, it is vital that we clear our minds of Western notions of atheism and theism. Westerners tend to think that someone who doesn't believe in a personal God (such as the Christian God) is an atheist.

This doesn't fit within Hinduism. Some Hindus believe in God as a personal god, as Krishna for example, but for others Brahman is 'pure consciousness' and not like 'a god' at all. This is important for RE teaching, because it expands our notion of 'ultimate reality' or what that thing called God might be like. Even young children can enjoy 'getting to grips' with this.

Vocabulary

Aum – a sacred symbol representing the sound of the ultimate reality.

Avatar – 'one who descends'; in this context this refers to manifestations of Vishnu, the two most important being Rama and Krishna.

Lingum – representation of Shiva, sometimes referred to as phallic.

Mantra – that which delivers the mind; a word, a short sacred text or a prayer that is said repetitiously.

Murti – 'form'; the image of a deity used in worship.

Shakti – feminine divine energy or power.

Upanishads – sacred texts that explain the meaning of the **Vedas**.

Vedas – from *veda* (knowledge); the four texts believed by Hindus to be revealed scriptures or shruti.

Yogi – someone who meditates; a contemplative who follows the jnana yoga of spiritual insight.

Sensitive issues

When teaching about Hinduism it is easy to give the wrong impression that Hindus are somehow primitive or mistaken in worshipping many gods.

It is important that the children understand that Hindus worship one God, not many murtis, and that they use the murtis as a focus for worship and a way of understanding an infinite God.

Amazing facts

In many parts of India a multitude of deities, animals and inanimate objects, such as stones, are used as a focus of worship. This is usually explained by identifying everything on earth with Brahman.

Common misconceptions

It is a common fallacy that Hindus 'worship idols'. In fact, the murti acts like an icon in Christianity. It is a form that enables worshippers to concentrate on the attributes of God. Murtis are sometimes referred to as 'windows into the divine'. The different images of God communicate the different attributes of Brahman.

Teaching ideas

● Set up a discussion or get the children to talk about how they understand God. What words would they use to describe God?
● Bring in a bell jar and ask the children if there is anything inside it. There is air, but we can't see it. What else is there but not seen?
● Look at how one person can be many things. For example, I am the author of this book but also a man, a father, a son, a brother, a teacher, a writer and so on. These are all different aspects of my nature but there is only one me!

Time, festivals and holy days

Subject facts

Time

For Hindus, time is cyclical; it has no starting point or end; it returns to the point where it began. Therefore the symbol of the wheel has become an important teaching tool in Hinduism. This view of time is very different from most Western views, which tend to see time and history as linear, with a starting point and an end point.

In the Hindu view of things, time is divided into a cycle of four **yugas** or ages. Westerners might use the term 'aeon'. Each one of these yugas is made up of thousands of years. The first yuga is called the sat yuga (the word 'sat' means a variety of things but can refer to reality or the true reality). It is a time of harmony and spiritual balance. The second and third yugas, dvapara yuga and treta yuga, represent a steady decline in spirituality, morality, justice and living standards. When the fourth yuga dawns, chaos reigns. This is the kali yuga or 'dark' yuga. This yuga will end when the tenth avatar of Vishnu intervenes to restore peace and stability to the universe. Then the cycle begins again and repeats itself infinitely.

One way of understanding this is to imagine Shiva Nataraj dancing the universe into motion. He is rather like the circus performer who spins plates. During the sat yuga the plate is revolving perfectly, but as time passes Shiva's dance tires and the plate begins to wobble, until ultimately it falls off the pole during the kali yuga. This is when Kali intervenes and destroys evil, and by doing this regenerates Shiva so that the dance can begin again.

Holy days and festivals

For Hindus, everyday life is also structured in circular fashion. To many Hindus all days are holy and time is marked by a myriad of festivals, feasts and celebrations. Each day of the week is associated with a different deity, for example Monday is Shiva's day and therefore a minor festival in itself for those who follow Shiva. There are also auspicious and inauspicious days for different things. For example, some Hindus will not travel on Fridays, but believe it is an auspicious day for the performance of some **pujas**, such as Lakshmi puja. Some months are auspicious for marriages.

The dates of most major festivals are based on the lunar calendar called the Panchang. The calendar is divided into 12 lunar months named after the stars in whose ascendancy the full moon of that month occurs. To account for the extra days of the solar year, there is an additional month (Adhik) every five years. Each month is divided into two parts, Shukla, the light fortnight, and Krishna, the dark fortnight. The bright half of the month is when the moon is increasing in size from the new-moon day until the full-moon day. The dark half of the month is when the moon is getting smaller, or becoming less bright, from full-moon day to new-moon day. The full-moon day in the middle of each month is very auspicious for Hindus and a Hindu festival is celebrated on each one.

Hindu festivals have a variety of characteristics and functions. Some are connected with nature and the seasons. Some are specifically religious and provide Hindus with a way of expressing their faith. Some festivals bring the community together, others remember key events in the history or mythology of the tradition. There are too many festivals to go into detail here, so three popular ones, **Diwali**, Krishna Janmashtami (Krishna's birthday) and Raksha Bandhan are briefly described.

Diwali

For many Hindus, Diwali is a time of great excitement. The word Diwali comes from Deepawali, meaning 'row' or 'cluster of lights', and Diwali is also known as the festival of lights. It takes place in the autumn and falls in the Hindu months of Asvina and Karthika (October and November).

There are many customs connected with Diwali, but two are considered most important. The first is the invitation of the goddess Lakshmi into each home: Lakshmi is welcomed with devas (little oil lamps) and rangoli patterns (designs made of coloured rice paste) on the floor at the entrance to the house. It is believed that Lakshmi's visit will bring good luck and prosperity to the house in the year to come. This is important because for many Hindus Diwali marks the beginning of a new financial year.

Secondly, Diwali celebrates the return home of Prince Rama and his wife Sita to **Ayodhya** after 14 years in exile. This story is recorded in the **Ramayana** – one of the great epics of Indian literature. Rama and Sita are held in great esteem, not only because Rama is an avatar of Vishnu, but also because he exemplifies the ideal way to fulfil one's **dharma**. Tradition records that on their return Rama and Sita were welcomed back by rows of lights. In modern times some Hindus replace the deva lamps with electric festival lights and hold firework displays.

Krishna Janmashtami

Krishna Janmashtami falls on the eighth day of the dark fortnight of Bhadrapada (August–September) and celebrates the midnight birth of Krishna in 3227BCE. For some Hindus, this is the most important festival of the year. Krishna as an avatar of Vishnu is perhaps the most popular of all Hindu deities and evokes great devotion from followers of the **bhakti** path (see page 80). For such people, Krishna personifies all that is right and good in human love, and reminds Hindus of the sublime love between God and humans.

Many Hindus fast for the whole day. Others make a partial fast, eating only fruit and milk. Temples are brightly decorated and throughout the day kirtan (religious songs) are sung, bells are rung and the conch shell is blown. Verses are recited from the Bhagavad Gita (see page 93) and stories of Krishna are told. Often, a cradle with an image of the baby Krishna is rocked at midnight, accompanied by offerings and repetitions of Krishna's mantra. In many temples, offerings of butter and curds are made at midnight, which remember Krishna's early years spent among the cowherds.

Raksha Bandhan

Raksha Bandhan falls on the full-moon day in the month of Shravana (July–August). Raksha means 'protection' and bhandhan means 'to tie'. On Raksha Bandhan, girls tie rakhis (bracelets of silk or cotton) on their brothers' wrists in order to bring blessings and good fortune to their brothers and to protect them from evil. In return, the brother promises to love, protect and care for his sister. This is a time of affirming family bonds. Nowadays many Hindus enclose rakhis in greeting cards. This means that these bonds can be affirmed from afar. Sometimes a woman may give a rakhi to a close male family friend. This symbolises that she sees the man as an adopted brother. It is a sign of sincere friendship and is a great honour.

As well as religious dharmas, there are family dharmas, such as the duty of parents to love their children and the duty of children to love and respect their parents and to provide emotional and financial support for them in their old age. Raksha Bandhan emphasises the dharma of a brother, which is to behave in a caring and affectionate way towards his sister, and a sister, who should behave in the same way towards her brother.

At Raksha Bandhan, men who wear the sacred thread (see pages 87–8) ceremonially remove the thread that they have worn for the past year and replace it with a new one.

Why you need to know these facts

The human desire to celebrate is common to all religions and learning about festivals is an important aspect of this. In Hinduism, the study of festivals can help children understand key concepts such as dharma or the nature of time and the universe. They are also a good way of learning the 'stories of the gods'.

Vocabulary

Ayodhya – a town in northern India believed to be the birthplace of Rama, and therefore a place of pilgrimage.
Bhakti yoga – the spiritual path of devotion.
Dharma – religious duty of a Hindu, based on the person's stage in life and social position.
Puja – worship.
Ramayana – Hindu epic relating the story of Rama and Sita.
Yuga – age; extended period of time. There are four yugas.

Amazing facts

India is so vast that a festival can be celebrated in different ways and at different times depending on what part of India it is taking place in. For example, different stories are told at Diwali depending on whether it is celebrated in the north or south. However, the symbolism of light and dark and good overcoming evil is a common thread.

Common misconceptions

Sikhs celebrate Diwali at the same time as Hindus, but their celebration remembers Guru Hargobind leading fellow captives out of prison (see page 208). Like Hindus, Sikhs celebrate Diwali with bonfires, clay devas and so on, and for Sikhs also, it celebrates the triumph of good over evil.

Teaching ideas

● Discuss what makes a particular time special. Make a chart of special times in the year suggested by the class.
● Explore ways in which we remember the past and the different ways in which we celebrate it.

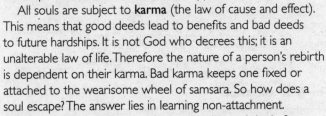

The journey and goal of life

Subject facts

The wheel of life

Hindus are born, live their lives, die and are cremated but, according to Hindu belief, this is not the end of the story. While the ashes of the body return to the earth, the **atman** (soul) is eternal and is born into another body which then continues its existence through another cycle. As the Hindu text the Bhagavad Gita says, death is like casting off one set of clothes and putting on new ones. This reincarnation is not seen as something to be joyful about; it is called **samsara** (the wearisome wheel of suffering and unsatisfactoriness). Therefore the aim for Hindus is to escape samsara and reach **moksha** (spiritual liberation).

All souls are subject to **karma** (the law of cause and effect). This means that good deeds lead to benefits and bad deeds to future hardships. It is not God who decrees this; it is an unalterable law of life. Therefore the nature of a person's rebirth is dependent on their karma. Bad karma keeps one fixed or attached to the wearisome wheel of samsara. So how does a soul escape? The answer lies in learning non-attachment.

What really hinders a soul from achieving moksha is, first of all, avidya (ignorance or blindness of spiritual truths); this, in turn, leads to maya (illusion about what really matters and what is really true). For example, spiritual blindness may lead a person to believe that material possessions will ultimately lead to happiness. This person would be lost in maya, as material things keep one attached to the world and so lead to more rebirths. Inappropriate attachments can also be emotional in nature –

the powerful emotions of love, hate, greed and selfishness all depend on a false view of who we are. Our ego-centredness and desire for things blinds us to our true nature – which lies beyond ego and ultimately rests in Brahman. According to Hindu belief, atman and Brahman are one and the same thing; the individual atman is like a droplet of water whose real place is in the ocean of Brahman. The trouble is that we don't realise this because of our self-centredness and blindness. The goal is to become a **sannyasin** or 'world renouncer'.

The three yogas

As mentioned above, Hinduism isn't really a fixed entity and includes a variety of spiritual paths. Moksha can be realised in different ways. These paths are called **yogas**.

● *Bhakti yoga* is the path of devotion to God. A devotee develops a loving relationship with a personal deity, such as Krishna, by devotion and worship and constantly keeping God in mind. By surrendering to the love of God, a person will be able to reach moksha.

● *Jnana yoga* is the path of spiritual insight and knowledge. In this path God is not realised as a personal deity but as an impersonal force. By meditating deeply, a devotee of this path is able to realize his or her oneness with Brahman.

● *Karma yoga* is the path of selfless service and action. A great example of this path was Mahatma Gandhi, who devoted his life to God through loving action towards others – especially those who were marginalized, such as the 'untouchables' – and non-violent action on behalf of social and political causes.

The four ashramas

A Hindu's spiritual journey follows the natural process of growing up. Life is divided into four stages or ashramas, each with its own dharma (spiritual duties).

● *Brahmacharya* is the first, or student, stage. This begins with the initiation of the sacred thread (see point 10 on pages 87–8) and has traditionally only been followed by the three upper varnas (see 'Sensitive issues' on pages 82). It involves following a dharma of gaining religious knowledge, especially of the Vedas (ancient scriptures). In the past, students would leave home between the ages of eight and 16 and go to the special school of a **guru**; today they attend conventional schools. However, it is still regarded as essential that a young person gains knowledge of the scriptures and develops appropriate attitudes towards teachers and parents.

● *Grihasta*, or householder, is the second stage. This stage centres on a dharma devoted to two of the aims of life for a Hindu, namely **artha** (earning one's living by honest means and providing for the family) and **kama** (enjoying the pleasures of life). Therefore a householder's dharma is focused on being a good husband or wife and a good parent. A householder's striving for moksha takes this very earthly form at this stage in their life.

● *Vanaprastha*, or retirement, is the third stage. This is a time when one's dharma switches from the more earthly matters of the householder to the more spiritual aims of non-attachment, meditation and study of the scriptures. Traditionally this stage begins when one's children have grown up and a son is born to the first son. This ensures the continuation of the family.

● *Sannyasin*, or world renouncer, is the final stage. This stage is not taken up by all Hindus, but is seen as an ideal. The sannyasin leaves home to become a wandering holy man with no fixed abode. All possessions are given up and a sannyasin concentrates solely on moksha. Many sannyasi can be found in India, often wandering from place to place, receiving their worldly needs, such as food, through the charity of others.

Why you need to know these facts

Getting to the heart of Hindu spirituality demands we know something of the Hindu view of life. The idea of a journey from birth to death that has its signposts and directions, in order that a person can get closer to achieving moksha, is an essential thing to understand. Such difficult ideas can best be presented to children in terms of the idea of a journey that encompasses different stages.

Hinduism

Vocabulary

Artha – earning one's living by honest means. One of the four aims of life for Hindus.

Atman – the real self, the soul, the divine spark of Brahman within all people.

Brahmins – priestly caste of Hinduism.

Guru – spiritual teacher; one who leads from darkness to light.

Kama – enjoying life's pleasures. One of the four aims in life for Hindus.

Karma – the law of cause and effect.

Moksha – liberation, freedom from the wheel of samsara.

Samsara – the world, the wearisome wheel, the place through which the soul passes in a series of rebirths.

Sannyasin – a world renouncer; a person in the fourth stage of life.

Yoga – spiritual path.

Sensitive issues

'Varna' refers to the original four 'castes' or sections of Hindu society. It was not a hierarchical structure. Each varna contributed to the whole. In the ancient text, the Rig Veda, society is likened to a human being with the **Brahmins** (priests) as the mouth, the Kshatriyas (administrators and warriors) as the arms, the Vaishyas (producers) as abdomen and thighs, and the Shudras (labourers) as feet that take the weight of society.

Originally the four varnas were equal and there were no 'untouchables'. Over time this system was altered and society became segregated and hierarchical, and many extra 'castes', called jatis, developed. These tended to be based on occupation and members of the upper castes considered those of the lower castes as inferior. Those who did 'unclean jobs', such as dealing with dead animals, were excluded from the varnas and were deemed 'untouchable'. There have been many attempts to reform the varna system, particularly by Mahatma Gandhi in the 1940s. Today, it is illegal to call someone 'untouchable'.

Common misconceptions

As many people today practise 'yoga', it is important to note several points in relation to learning about Hinduism. Firstly, yoga is not the same as meditation and nor is it merely a set of physical exercises. 'Yoga' comes from the Hindu word *yolk* and means to unite, connect, or establish a relationship with the Supreme Being or ultimate reality. Meditation, however, need not be focused on a divine reality at all.

Teaching ideas

- Explore the idea of life as a journey and plot on the line where the children are now. How would they describe their particular stage in terms of their dharma or duties?
- Explore with the class what makes them happy and sad. How does it feel when you feel free? What are negative and positive feelings?
- Discuss the three yogas. Visit a temple to learn about Bhakti yoga. Do some basic meditation (breath counting) to learn about Jnana yoga. Watch a suitable part of the film *Gandhi* (1982) to learn about Karma yoga. Get the children to write about the type of yoga that would best suit them.
- Discuss what the children would like to achieve when they grow up.

Key values

Subject facts

The most common examples of Hindu ethics are known as the niyamas (observances) and the yamas (abstentions). These form part of a spiritual path called Raj Yoga.

The five niyamas are:

Shaucha – be pure in mind, body and speech.
Santosh – seek contentment; be satisfied with what you have.
Tapa – be prepared to make sacrifices; be patient and calm under stress.
Svadhyaya – study the scriptures.
Ishwarapranidhan – worship daily and cultivate devotion.

The five yamas are:

Ahimsa – reverence for all living things (see below).
Satya – refrain from lying; seek the truth.
Asteya – do not steal.
Brahmacharya – avoid lust and intoxicants.
Aparigraha – avoid desire and greed.

Ahimsa

Because of the belief that Brahman is present in all living things, there is a great emphasis on non-violence in Hinduism. The key concept here is one of ahimsa (reverence for all living things). This value is at its strongest in the Jain tradition. Amongst Jains, ahimsa is an expression of a whole way of life. It is ritualised, especially by monks who wear a gauze mask, strain all drinks and brush the path in front of them in order to avoid harming any living creature. In the Hindu tradition in general, it finds expression in vegetarianism and protecting cows. Not all Hindus are vegetarian but vegetarian food is regarded as the most pure and most appropriate for special occasions. It is true to say that this principle of harmlessness can be seen as a thread running through all aspects of Hindu life. Mahatma Gandhi strongly emphasised ahimsa, reinterpreting it to mean not only avoiding harm to others, but also positively pursuing it in relationships with others and developing it into his philosophy of non-violent political action.

Why you need to know these facts

The value of ahimsa is a key concept in understanding the Hindu view of life. The values described here are the essence of Sanatan Dharma (the eternal way). Therefore, it is important to include some explicit teaching about these values to reflect accurately the Hindu tradition.

Vocabulary

Ahimsa – reverence for all living things; not killing; non-violence; respect for life. A key Hindu value practised especially by Jains.
Jainism – an Indian religious movement whose key figure was Mahavira (599–527BCE), the last of the Jain tirthankaras (ford makers) who taught the way to liberation from physical bondage to the world.
Sanatan Dharma – 'the eternal way'; most Hindus prefer this title for their religion.

Amazing facts

In India, cows roam all over the place, even on main roads! They are regarded as sacred, in some cases even as deities, because they provide all the basic needs of life. Some cows are looked after by temple priests.

Common misconceptions

While ahimsa is often associated with non-violence and vegetarianism, it does not only refer to these aspects. A true understanding of ahimsa involves abstaining from evil in terms of word and thought as well as deed.

- Explore positive and negative attitudes and feelings towards others. Discuss in what way negative attitudes can be harmful.
- Read about the life of Ghandhi.
- Learn about Jain monks and the practice of ahimsa in this tradition.

Samskars

Subject facts

Samskars are acts of purifying, refining and developing the body and mind. They are performed at significant stages in a person's life and provide direction along the journey of life from birth to death. The 16 samskars are:

1. *Garbhahana.* This is performed after the wedding ceremony, at the time of the menstruation of the new bride. A prayer is said for the continuation of the human race and the conception and fertilisation of a garbha (embryo).

2. *Punasavana.* This is performed during the second or third month of pregnancy. Prayers are said to ensure healthy physical growth of the baby.

3. *Simantonnayana.* This is performed during the sixth or eighth month of pregnancy. Prayers are said to ensure the healthy mental development of the baby.

4. *Jatakarma.* The new-born is welcomed into the world by putting a small amount of honey on its tongue. A prayer is also whispered into the baby's ear – 'May the God the creator of all things grant you firm wisdom. Knowledge and wisdom are the sources of power and long life.'

5. *Namakaran.* The naming ceremony. This is performed about 11 days after birth. The mother may well have her first bath after giving

birth, the father will shave for the first time after the birth and the house will be filled with fresh flowers. These are all rituals of purification and symbols of new life. The priest will cast a horoscope for the child to determine the first letter of the child's name. It is tradition that names are meaningful. For example, a boy might be called Bimal (pure), Rajiv (lotus, the symbol of enlightenment) or Krishna after the deity. A girl might be called Parvati (the consort of Shiva), Chandra (moon) or Hetal (friendly).

6. *Nishkramana.* This is often referred to as the child's first outing, or the child's introduction to nature. It usually occurs when the child is about four months old, when he or she is exposed to the rays of the Sun. The father performs puja (worship) at the shrine at home and says special prayers to the family deities.

7. *Annaprashana.* This coincides with teething and is concerned with the child's first solid food. The father performs puja and the baby is spoon-fed some rice mixed with yoghurt, ghee and honey.

8. *Choodakarma* or *Mundan.* The child's first haircut. This takes place between the ages of one and three. The child's head is completely shaved. In India, this can take place anywhere, often in the open air. In Britain, the ceremony is more likely to be performed at the local mandir (temple). It is symbolic of purification and the removing of bad karma from the previous life. It is also an opportunity to check the health of the scalp and that the skull is joining at the fontanelle.

9. *Karnavedha.* Traditionally this marks a Brahmin boy's ears being pierced between the ages of three and five. Today, it is more popular amongst girls and it is often performed on the day of the naming ceremony.

10. *Upanayana.* The sacred thread ceremony. This is the initiation of boys from the three upper varnas into the brahmacharya (student) stage of life (see pages 80–1). Upanayana means getting closer to someone, in this case the boy is getting closer to his guru (teacher). During the ceremony, the boy wears white to symbolise purity. The father places the thread on the boy who vows to be celibate during his student stage and to take seriously his dharma, which largely involves the study of the scriptures. The

sacred thread (yajnopaveet) has three strands which symbolise three obligations:

- *Rish Rin.* The obligation to promote knowledge gained from all sages, thinkers and scientists.
- *Pitri Rin.* The obligation to look after and respect one's parents and ancestors.
- *Dev Rin.* The obligation towards the society and nation in which one lives.

11. *Vedarambha.* The start of formal education; from 'veda' (knowledge) and 'ambha' (start). Traditionally, students went to live with their teacher at a boarding school from the age of 12 until they were 24 years old.

12. *Samavartana.* The graduation ceremony marking the end of formal studies. It includes various ceremonies involving the use of water and the student is eventually garlanded. The student is now ready to participate fully in society.

13. *Vivaha.* The marriage ceremony. This samskara marks the beginning of the second ashrama, grihasta ashrama (see page 81). Two people who are considered suitable for a lifelong marriage are given explanations of the duties and responsibilities of a householder.

14. *Vanaprastha.* A ceremony to mark the beginning of the third ashrama, vanaprastha ashrama (see page 81). This usually takes place at about age 60.

15. *Sannyasin.* A ceremony to mark the beginning of the fourth ashrama, sannyasin ashrama (see page 81).

16. *Antyeshti.* The death rites.

Marriage

Marriage in Hindu tradition is not simply the joining of two individuals but also of two families. Therefore, the question of whether a marriage is suitable is normally considered in this wider context. If the boy and girl come from the same varna, and therefore share a common culture, they are more likely to be able to make a secure marriage.

The parents normally arrange the marriage. Even when a boy and girl have dated each other, the parents have a great deal of say about whether the marriage takes place or not. However, in urban India and Britain, where Hindu girls have more opportunities to meet boys, parents are increasingly under pressure to accept their children's choice. If the boy and girl are of the same background and religion, parents may be willing to give their consent.

There are normally seven stages to this samskara, but two are considered essential: the **kanyadaan**, the giving away of the bride, and the **saptapadi** ceremony, in which the betrothed couple take seven steps together.

Kanyadaan

The father of the bride formally gives his daughter to the bridegroom, asking him to cherish and love her. He takes his daughter's hand and offers it to the groom, who accepts his new bride. At this time, the bride's parents traditionally offer a dowry – a share of the family property given in the form of jewellery, new clothes and household goods. However, what began as a voluntary gift became an obligation, causing families great hardship. For this reason, the payment of dowry to the groom's parents has been declared illegal in India. However, the practice still continues.

The betrothed couple sit facing each other, separated at first by a silk curtain. They then sit side by side in front of the sacred fire (agni). The bride's sari is tied to the groom's garment to symbolically join them. While the officiating priest recites sacred verses, the couple make offerings of ghee (clarified butter) and rice to the sacred fire. The bride and groom hold hands and circle the fire while the groom makes a pledge of friendship and commitment.

Saptapadi

The most important stage of the wedding ceremony is saptapadi, when the bride and groom take the seven steps around the sacred fire, or walk in a circle around the fire seven times. As they do this, the priest recites mantras from the Vedas and the bride and groom recite:

Let us pray together,
For life-power, as we tread two steps together,
For wealth more abundant, as we go on three steps with
*   one another,*
For happiness in life, as we walk four steps together,
For offspring, as we move along five steps together,
For a long-wedded life, as we pledge six steps together,
Be thou my life-mate as we walk up seven steps together,
Thus do thou go together with me for ever and ever,
Let us thus acquire many, many sons, and long may they live,
*   we pray.*

The large group of family members and friends who are usually invited to be at the wedding blesses the couple. A feast follows and a reception is held in the evening.

Funerals

The funeral rites are of great importance. They are performed to bring peace to the soul of the departed and to bring comfort to the bereaved.

Antyeshti, the last samskara, is performed at death. The precise customs vary depending on family tradition, caste, and region. Most Hindus prefer to die at home, surrounded by family members. When death is near, a drop of holy water is usually put into the dying person's mouth and passages are read from the scriptures.

When the person has died, funeral preparations begin. In Britain, the body might be taken to the undertaker and ceremonies may be performed in the chapel. In India, if the person dies in hospital the body is usually brought home. It is washed by one of the family members, anointed with sandalwood paste, wrapped in a new white cloth and laid on the floor in the sitting room. The family members, including the children, view the body. A small lamp is lit to guide the departed soul on its journey. Relatives and friends visit the bereaved family to offer condolences and some stay with the family during the mourning period.

When children, sannyasi (see page 81) and others who are outside the ritual system die, they are normally buried; everyone else is usually cremated. The cremation usually takes place on the same day the person dies, but it may be delayed to await family members from abroad.

The eldest son or the nearest male relative performs the last rites. He lights the pyre, first at the north end and then at other points until it is totally ablaze. After the body has been completely reduced to ashes, the mourners bathe to remove their ritual defilement. On the third day, they return to the funeral ground, collect the ashes and scatter them in the Ganges or another sacred river. Some Hindus in Britain send the ashes to India to be immersed in the Ganges.

A mourning period of ten to 12 days follows. Hindus perform an annual memorial ceremony, shraddha, on the anniversary of the death.

Why you need to know these facts

This subject matter is important in its connections with the human experience category of stages of life. All children can relate to important stages in their life and therefore understand these samskars better.

Vocabulary

Kanyadaan – a ceremony in which the bride is given away during the marriage ceremony.
Saptapadi – a ceremony in which the married couple take seven steps together.

Amazing facts

Certain elements of the samskars can be traced back in time as far as 2000BCE.

Common misconceptions

Although there are 16 samskars, and some scriptures mention 40, it is probably only necessary to concentrate on five: the naming, the first outing, the sacred thread ceremony, marriage and death. Many Hindus do not see all 16 as being relevant to modern life and only orthodox Brahmin males experience all 16 samskars.

Teaching ideas

- Talk about the ways in which we learn to do more things for, and by, ourselves.
- Discuss how growing older and bigger can provide opportunities to do new things, including taking on new responsibilities.
- Explore the children's thoughts and feelings about the fact that all things come to an end. Look in nature for signs of decay and rebirth.

Sacred scriptures

Subject facts

To the uninitiated, the Hindu tradition might seem like an unfathomable and complicated tradition with many scriptures! To make matters easier it is important to understand that Hindu scriptures can be classified under two headings: **shruti** and **smriti**.

Shruti

The shruti (revealed truths) are scriptures believed to have been revealed to holy men who interpreted them for those who seek spiritual guidance. They are ancient and contain the scriptures referred to as the Vedas and the Upanishads.

Smriti

The smriti (remembered truths) form what is usually referred to as the popular religious literature of the tradition. The smriti contain the great Hindu epics, such as the Ramayana and the **Mahabharata**, and the later scriptures called the **Puranas**. The stories contained in these scriptures address the religious beliefs, ideals and values of the Hindu way of life. The most famous section of the Mahabharata is the Bhagavad Gita. The 'Gita' is a conversation between Arjuna, who is preparing to fight a battle, and his charioteer, who is in fact Lord Krishna. The Gita teaches that devotion to God (bhakti yoga – see page 80) is the highest form of worship. This explains its great popularity amongst many Hindus. The Ramayana, which contains the story of Rama and Sita, contains the universal message that good triumphs over evil. Many teachers will be familiar with this story as it is recited during the festival of Diwali. Finally, the Puranas tell the stories of the gods. The most popular, the Bhagavad Purana, tells of Vishnu (see pages 70–1) and his avatars, including Krishna. The Puranas also tell of the other main Hindu gods, Brahma and Shiva (see pages 70 and 71–2).

Why you need to know these facts

The literature of Hinduism is vast but important for teaching purposes. It is important to understand the difference between shrutis and smritis. Although both are extremely important, it is the smritis, that are most appropriate for primary teaching. In effect, the stories deal with the practical application of the 'eternal principles' contained in the more ancient shruti.

Vocabulary

Mahabharata – scripture that includes the Bhagavad Gita.
Puranas – part of the smriti scriptures; contains many well-known Hindu stories.
Shruti – revealed truths; refers particularly to the Vedas.
Smriti – remembered truths; applied to epics such as the Mahabharata and Ramayana.

Amazing facts

The famous writer Max Muller referred to the Vedas as the oldest books in the library of humankind. Hindus believe that the content of the Vedas was revealed by God at the beginning of creation.

Common misconceptions

Hinduism is not like the Western traditions of Judaism, Christianity and Islam in having essentially one authoritative scripture. Although the Vedas have great authority in Hinduism it is a tradition of great diversity. It is true that the Bhagavad Gita occupies a special place in many Hindus' lives but it is not on account of any special authority.

Teaching ideas

Information about the sacred scriptures themselves is not as important at this stage as what they contain. Children need to hear appropriate stories from the smriti. A good place to start is with stories from the Puranas. For example:

- The birth of Krishna
- Krishna as a boy
- How Ganesh received his elephant head
- The birth of the Ganges
- Why Shiva has a third eye

It is possible to obtain colourful copies of the Bhagavad Gita for classroom use.

Pilgrimage

Subject facts

The Sanskrit word for a place of pilgrimage is **tirtha**, meaning crossing place or ford. Most places of pilgrimages are located on the banks of holy rivers, in particular the Ganges, Hindus' most sacred river. In traditional Indian spiritual thought, a pilgrimage enables the pilgrim to cross the symbolic river of life to the shore of spiritual liberation or moksha, where the pilgrim can be united with the divine and released from the cycle of rebirth.

Water is considered by Hindus to be one of the primordial elements from which all things in the universe are created. To bathe in the waters of the holy Ganges, for example, is believed to be like bathing in **amrit**, the original water that gave life to all creation. Bathing in the river is seen as purifying, washing away all sins and sanctifying. Like all rivers, the Ganges is believed to have a divine origin and it is considered to be the holiest of rivers. It is regarded as the Mother Goddess, **Ganga Ma**, who nourishes and sustains all life, especially those who come seeking her favour.

There are many reasons why a Hindu may decide to go on pilgrimage. Hindus may undertake a pilgrimage to withdraw from everyday life for a while in order to concentrate fully on spiritual matters and to gain religious merit. The focus of such a pilgrimage may be to have a **darshan** (glimpse) of the deity and receive **prasad** (blessed food). In the process of pilgrimage a person may bathe in a holy river, seek spiritual counselling from gurus or other holy people and visit many temples, or a particular famous temple.

People may go on pilgrimage in order to obtain divine assistance with some problem or situation in daily life. A pilgrim may be fulfilling a vow to a deity whose blessing they have asked for. The blessing may be to help the pilgrim with an illness or with personal or family problems. People may also go on pilgrimage in connection with one of the samskars (see pages 86–8).

Many places in India are considered holy by Hindus, but the two most important holy sites are the cities of Varanasi and Hardwar.

Varanasi

Varanasi is situated at the mouth of the river Ganges in North-Eastern India and is one of the oldest cities in the world. Since ancient times it has been a centre of religious life and tradition, of pilgrimage, of Hindu culture and learning. It is sometimes called Benares by Westerners. The old name for the city is Kashi, which means 'resplendent with divine light'. This is particularly evident in the early morning beside the river Ganges.

Varanasi is a busy city dedicated to Shiva. It has an important Hindu university and many temples dedicated to Shiva. At the centre of the city is the river Ganges and the pilgrims who come to worship. All human life can be experienced at the **ghats** alongside the river. Many people bring the bodies of their dead relatives to be cremated by the side of India's holiest river. Ganges water is used all over the world in worship and rituals.

Hardwar

The ancient city of Hardwar is considered to be holy for many reasons, firstly because it is located where the holy river Ganges comes down from the Himalayas in northern India. **Vaishnavites** (devotees of Vishnu) and **Shaivites** (devotees of Shiva) have different explanations for the origins of the river Ganges. Vaishnavites say that the Ganges flowed from the foot of Vishnu. A particularly holy place for them is the ghat called Har Ki Pauri where the Ganges touches what they believe to be the footprint of Vishnu. The Shaivites say that the Ganges flowed down from heaven through the hair of Shiva.

Hardwar is full of wandering ascetics, holy men and astrologers whom pilgrims can consult for advice. Priests are available to help pilgrims to perform religious ceremonies, sometimes on behalf of relatives. There are many ashrams (places of spiritual retreat) where pilgrims can stay. There are also ashrams whose primary purpose is to help Hindus lead a holy life, to educate them and to assist them to bring about social justice. Because Hardwar is a holy city, meat and alcohol are not available.

Hardwar is one of the four cities where the **Kumbha Mela** (pitcher fair) – the largest and most important of the pilgrimage festivals – is held every 12 years. Stories tell how the gods had been victims of a curse and wanted to regain their strength by drinking amrit, the nectar of life. The gods and demons fought over the amrit and the gods won the struggle. When one of the gods, in the form of a bird, took the amrit to heaven, it spilled in four places: Naskit, Ujjain, Prayag (Allahabad) and Hardwar. The four cities host the Kumbha Mela in turn.

Why you need to know these facts

The idea of pilgrimage is common to many religious traditions and there are clear connections between religious pilgrimage and a special journey. Most importantly, though, the connection between Hindu pilgrimage and human experience in general is the notion of life as a journey, because ultimately Hindus go on pilgrimage to achieve moksha (spiritual liberation). Therefore, when teaching about Hindu pilgrimage it is important to concentrate on *why* people go on pilgrimage.

Vocabulary

Amrit – holy water.
Darshan – a glimpse of a deity.
Ganga Ma – the Mother Goddess; the holy River Ganges.
Ghat – In India, a flight of steps leading down to a river or landing place. On the Ganges at Varanasi one of these ghats is used for funerals, hence the term 'funeral ghat'.
Kumbha Mela – the largest and most important Hindu pilgrimage festival, held every 12 years.
Prasad – blessed food.
Shaivite – devotee of Shiva.
Tirtha – a place of pilgrimage.
Vaishnavite – devotee of Vishnu.

Amazing facts

Nearly 30 million people, including religious leaders, ascetics, priests, gurus and their disciples, and millions of pilgrims, usually attend the Kumbha Mela. It is the largest gathering of any kind in the world.

Common misconceptions

A pilgrimage is not a holiday but a serious spiritual journey.

Teaching ideas

● Apart from the two places described in detail, there are many other places on which you could choose to focus your work. For example, the holy sites of Vrindavan and Ayodhya, which are connected with Krishna and Rama respectively.
● Read stories connected with pilgrimage, for example the story of Rama and Sita or the descent of the Ganges.
● Explore the places that children travel to and identify the reasons for travel.

Worship

Subject facts

For Hindus, worship is not a corporate activity but an individual expression of devotion, although it is true to say that worship in the temple does tend to be more congregational in Britain than it is in India.

Worship in the home

Most Hindu homes have a special place where puja (worship) is performed. The things needed to perform puja are kept in this area along with murtis of one or more deities and Hindu symbols, such as the swastika or the aum symbol. There will also be an incense holder and bell.

Before performing puja, a Hindu will have a bath so as to be cleansed to appear before God. The Hindu begins puja by ringing a bell to gain the attention of the deity. He or she will light incense sticks to purify the air and provide a pleasant-smelling atmosphere. The devotee will then say a number of prayers, always including the Gayatri Mantra. He or she will make offerings to the deity, which may be water, milk or foods such as fruit, rice, nuts or sweets. Sometimes the murti is bathed and dressed. A lamp might be lit and the **aarti** ceremony performed – this is an offering of light in a circular motion to the deities; it is an act of reverence and devotion to the many forms of the Divine. Light in the form of agni (fire) symbolises purification; light is also seen as the mediator between God and humankind. During the performance of puja, a devotee may make a mark on his or her forehead with kum kum or sandalwood paste. This is known as the tilak mark and symbolises the 'third eye' of spiritual wisdom.

The performance of puja can take a very long time. However, if a devotee's time is short, he or she might just light an incense stick and say a quick prayer. Hindus believe that even the shortest prayer is acceptable to God.

Worship in the temple

In Britain, the local Hindu community may come together at the mandir (temple) at the weekend. Usually there is an aarti service each day in the morning and again in the evening. As well as places of worship, many Hindu temples are also community centres.

All temples have a priest whose main function is to look after the murtis. Each day he ritually awakens and washes them, usually with a combination of water and milk. He then dresses them in clothes that have been donated by a Hindu family.

The priests will also offer light during the morning and evening aarti ceremonies. When aarti takes place in the temple, the priest offers the light to the deities and then brings it down amongst the worshippers. The worshippers usually pass their hands over the flame and then touch their foreheads to bring the blessing of light to themselves. In some temples, holy water is also distributed to the worshippers. A small amount of water is placed in the hand of the worshipper who then may drink it or put it on their forehead or in their hair. Puja always concludes with the distribution of prasad (blessed food). In many temples this is a piece of fruit or sweets.

Why you need to know these facts

Although there are many forms of worship in Hinduism, it is best to focus on worship in the home and worship in the temple. As mentioned on page 98, Hindu worship isn't essentially congregational and devotees can worship in many ways. The popular Bhakti tradition (see page 80) is really what is being described here – worshipping God and the qualities of God through murtis. It would be too complicated to go into great detail about other forms of worship but it is important that the teacher knows something about them. These are:

● *Jnana yoga*. Worshipping God as having no qualities or form; God as pure consciousness in which the worshipper transcends his or her own ego.

● *Karma yoga*. Worshipping God as having qualities such as compassion, knowledge and so on, but no form.

Vocabulary

Aarti – a ceremony in which light is offered to the deities and then offered to the devotees.

Sensitive issues

When visiting an aarti ceremony at a Hindu temple, all present are welcome to 'take the light' as the aarti lamp is brought down to the devotees. Don't be put off by this. No one will be offended if you decline. Usually devotees drop some loose change into the tray before taking the light. You may feel more comfortable doing this. Nevertheless it is worth pointing out that in taking the light you are, essentially, receiving a blessing from the divine – however you understand it!

Common misconceptions

First, look again at the 'Common misconceptions' section on page 74. It is also worth noting that in India a temple is likely to be dedicated to a particular aspect of the divine, for example it will be a Shiva or Vishnu temple. However, it is common in Britain for temples to house murtis of both Vishnu and Shiva. This is because there might be only one temple for a diverse Hindu community.

Teaching ideas

- Visit a Hindu temple and attend the aarti ceremony.
- 'Build' a shrine in the classroom and dedicate it to a particular murti.
- Learn some of the Hindu prayers, like the aarti hymn, the Gayatri Mantra, or the prayer for peace.
- Write some acrostic poems on light, aarti or mandir.
- Create a poster to advertise an aarti ceremony.
- Design a booklet intended for first-time visitors to a Hindu temple.
- Collect artefacts such as a puja tray (available from most religious artefact suppliers).
- Introduce the children to the murti of Ganesh (the remover of obstacles). Get them to write a letter to Ganesh asking for obstacles in their own lives to be removed.

Resources

Artefacts suppliers

Gohil Emporium (Indian Arts and Crafts), 381 Stratford Road, Birmingham B11 4JZ, 0121 771 3048, **www.gohilemporium.co.uk** Mail order service available.
Religion in Evidence (see page 33 for details).
Articles of Faith (see page 33 for details).

Iskcon Educational Services, Bhaktivedanta Manor,
Hilfield Lane, Aldenham, Watford, Hertfordshire
WD25 8EZ, 01923 859 578, http://ies.iskcon.org

TV programmes (available on DVD)

Channel 4 *Animated World Faiths* series for ages 7–11.
Channel 4 *Stop, Look, Listen*, 'Water, Moon, Candle, Tree and
Sword'. Suitable for KS1 children.

Useful books

Religion in Focus: Hinduism by Geoff Teece (Franklin Watts, 2008).
Create and Display: Festivals by Claire Tinker (Scholastic, 2010).

Useful websites

www.hindunet.org
http://ies.iskcon.org
www.bbc.co.uk/schools/religion/hinduism
www.reonline.org.uk
http://retoday.org.uk

Islam

It is often said that Islam began with the Prophet Muhammad (570–632CE). The Prophet Muhammad is sometimes referred to as the 'founder' of Islam. Both these statements are incorrect. Muslims believe that God had been revealing his message over many centuries and had been sending his **rasul** (messenger) to various parts of the world to preach the same truth. Therefore Muslims believe that all prophets, going back to Adam, preached the same **din** (religion). However, this guidance was often corrupted and so God sent further prophets to restate the original purity of the revelation. Muslims, therefore, affirm writings such as the Torah (of Prophet Musa or Moses) and the Gospels (of Prophet Isa or Jesus) but believe them to be corrupted forms of the original revelation. Accordingly, Muslims believe that the final and most comprehensive form of God's message was revealed to the Prophet Muhammad and is enshrined in the Qur'an. Consequently, Muslims do not believe that the Prophet Muhammad brought a new faith into the world. Sometimes called the 'seal of the prophets', the Prophet Muhammad came to complete the series of prophets who had brought God's message over time to the people of the world. The Prophet Muhammad is more accurately seen as the last prophet of Islam rather than the first!

Part of people's confusion about this lies in the way the terms *islam* and *muslim* are used. In Western thinking, *Islam* describes a religion that evolved in the Middle East in the 6th century and *Muslim* a person who follows that religion. Therefore, Islam is one religion within a series of religions that include, for example all the religions described in this book and more. However, Islamic teaching doesn't really see it like this. The word *islam* is a concept, which means 'the attainment of peace through submission to the will of God'. A *muslim* is one who submits. Therefore all who submit to the will of the one true God are muslims. Consequently, Muslims believe that there is only one religion, the religion of Islam, which God has revealed since time began. Does this mean, therefore, that Muslims should accept all other religions as God-given? Not exactly. Whilst Islam teaches that all the prophets preached the same fundamentals, in the cases of religions such as Judaism and Christianity, the followers of these traditions have 'gone astray' and suppressed, added to, or altered the original message. The Muslim attitude to other religions is therefore to invite others to return to the 'purest' form of God's message. If this is not acceptable to followers of other religions then it is the duty of a Muslim to pursue good and harmonious relations with people of other traditions, as long as they do not abuse Islam.

There are an estimated 1.7 billion Muslims worldwide. In Britain, there has been a Muslim presence since the early 19th century, but it wasn't until the 1960s that the community grew much larger. Today, there are over 2 million Muslims in Britain, with sizeable communities in the West Midlands, West Yorkshire, Lancashire, London and Scotland. In Birmingham alone, there are more than 100 mosques. It is the second largest religion in the United Kingdom.

The majority of Muslims in the UK are British-born with family origins in Pakistan, India and Bangladesh. There are significant numbers of Cypriot, Turkish and Yemeni Muslims, together with more recently settled refugees from Afghanistan, Iran, Iraq, Bosnia, Somalia and Albania. There are also a growing number of Muslims of Afro-Caribbean and European origin, and a significant number of indigenous Britons have embraced Islam. A diverse community therefore means that a number of different languages are spoken, from the sub-continent languages of Urdu, Punjabi and Gujarati, to Turkish and Malay. However, Muslims consider it an important skill to be able to read Arabic because it is the language of the Qur'an.

The sections that follow are based around four key concepts: tawhid (oneness of God, Allah), iman (faith), ibadah (worship) and akhlaq (character and moral conduct).

When Muslims say the Prophet Muhammad's name (or the name of any other prophet) they say, 'Peace be upon him,' as a mark of respect.

God (Allah) and humanity

A Muslim's belief in God is expressed most simply and clearly in
the Shahadah, the Muslim statement of faith:

> *I bear witness that there is no god but Allah and I bear witness
> that Muhammad is His messenger.*
>
> The Shahadah

It is the first duty of Muslims to make this declaration of faith. The
Shahadah is usually printed over the **qiblah** wall in a mosque; it is
contained in the first words whispered into a new-born baby's
ear and the last words uttered by a dying person.

The Shahadah affirms a Muslim's belief in tawhid (oneness of
God). This belief is the basis for all other beliefs. As the Qur'an
puts it:

> *No son did God beget, nor is there any god along
> with Him.*
>
> Surah 23:91

Indeed the very idea of anything in the world being worshipped
apart from Allah, or compared to Him, is a great sin, called
shirk. Allah creates everything in the universe and only Allah is
uncreated. Nothing happens in the world that is not willed by
Allah – Muslims refer to this as **qadar** (Allah's complete control
over everything). As it says in the Qur'an:

> *He is God, the only God, on whom all depend. He begetteth not,
> nor is He begotten, and there is none like Him.*
>
> Surah 112:1–4

God's attributes

According to Islam, the essence of God is beyond all attributes
or qualities through which human beings try and understand
him. The relationship between the absolute qualities of Allah

and human beings can be understood by looking at the creation of the first human, Adam. The Qur'an tells us that when Allah created Adam, he breathed something absolute into a creature that is contingent, in other words subservient to the laws of nature, of death and decay. We are told that Allah taught Adam the names of all things. In effect this means that human beings were given conceptual understanding of the world around them.

The essence of all created things reflects an attribute of God, that humans, uniquely amongst creatures, have been given the ability to comprehend the attributes of God. The attributes of God are perfect and eternal. They provide for human beings the perfect, absolute norm for mercy, justice, truth, goodness, beauty and so on. We all have the potential for these attributes and should try to develop them.

Muslims refer to the implanting within the heart of Adam the potential to understand the attributes of God as 'trust'. This trust enables humans to see the beauty of God in a flower, for example, or the power of God in a thunderstorm, or the grandeur and infinite nature of God in the sky. Therefore, even though we are earthly creatures who are susceptible to 'taking on' the qualities of the world and becoming prey to tendencies we share with the animal kingdom, such as greed, passion, selfishness or cruelty, our real, absolute nature remains. True, it is often hidden from us, and the tension between the absolute and contingent selves can cause perpetual conflict within a person. However, a life of submission to Allah, following the guidance of the Prophet Muhammad, will enable human beings to realise the God-given qualities within and become a qalb (a person with harmony of heart). He or she will become a peace-loving **mujahid** (one who fights for Allah).

Humankind is told in the Qur'an to:

> Call upon God or call upon **Rahman**, by whatever Name, you call upon Him (it is well). For to Him belong the most Beautiful Names.

Surah 17: 110

These names are the attributes of God that Muslims need to remember, study and meditate upon. The Prophet Muhammad said:

There are 99 names that are Allah's alone. Whoever learns, understands and enumerates them enters Paradise and achieves eternal salvation.

The **Hadith**

It is believed that the hundredth name is hidden from humankind because, despite being created with God-given qualities, God remains beyond any human's comprehension. Human beings can approach God but cannot identify themselves with God.

Why you need to know these facts

Understanding Muslim ideas about God and humanity's relationship to God is the basis on which we can understand the life of a Muslim. As, according to Muslim belief, everything depends on God, seeing life through the eyes of a Muslim must include understanding what Muslims believe about God. In religious education we have the opportunity to introduce children to different ideas about God, and help them to clarify their own ideas about this central component of religious belief. As a summary it is worth exploring with the children the ideas: that God is the most important thing in the universe; that God is just and kind; that people should live as God commands; and that God cannot be thought of in human terms.

Vocabulary

Din – obedience; submission; religion. Islam (submission to God) is regarded in the Qur'an as al-din – the religion.
Hadith – a tradition or narration relating or describing a saying or an action of the Prophet.
Mujahid – one who 'fights' in the path of Allah.
Qadar – Allah's complete and final control over the fulfilment of events or destiny.
Qiblah – direction in which Muslims face when praying.
Rahman – God the merciful.
Rasul – messenger of Allah.
Sufi – a Muslim mystic.

Sensitive issues

You will not find any representations of God in the Qur'an, a mosque or a Muslim home. It is not permissible to 'illustrate' God because he is greater than humans can imagine and because of the danger of idolatry. Be careful, then, not to store, for example, Muslim artefacts with representations of Hindu deities. Also, don't get children to draw God in the context of teaching about Islam. Descriptions, however, are perfectly permissible.

Amazing facts

There is a tragic case of a **Sufi** mystic, Mansur al-Hajj, being executed for saying 'ana al-Haqq' ('I am the truth' or 'I am God'). Sufis try to 'keep alive' the inward, spiritual aspects of Islam known as tariqah. Their goal is to lose ego and achieve a state called fana (self-noughting) and so become 'full' of the characteristics of God. Obviously some Muslims at the time believed Mansur al-Hajj had gone too far in identifying himself with God.

Common misconceptions

Some Westerners perceive the Muslim idea of God to be very authoritarian and judgemental. While Allah is the greatest authority for Muslims, obedience to God's will results in great compassion and mercy emanating from God. God is inexorably involved in people's lives and cares so much that even a sinner at death is not confined to hell for eternity. All have a chance to repent. Muslims will point to this as one example of the mercy of God.

Teaching ideas

● Look at and discuss the purpose of Muslim prayer beads. Research the 99 names of God. Give the children round pieces of card and get them to write a name on a card and decorate it.

Thread them together in the form of a rosary and hang it in the classroom.
● Together, create a list of the ways in which Muslims believe that God helps people.
● Explore ways in which people feel they get messages from God in nature. For example: black clouds and rain; leaves turning in autumn; buds in spring. Get the children to think of one example and illustrate it.

Messengers of Allah

Subject facts

As we noted in the introduction, Muslims believe that Allah has revealed the same message of faith throughout all time, and that the message has been preached to humanity by the prophets of Allah. The Prophet Muhammad is believed to be the last in the line of prophets. The Qur'an names 25 prophets beginning with Adam and including Nuh (Noah), Ibrahim (Abraham), Ishmail (Ishmael), Yaqub (Jacob), Ayyub (Job), Musa (Moses), Dawud (David), Suleiman (Solomon), Yahya (John) and Isa (Jesus).

Muslims believe, however, that there have been many more prophets (either 140,000 or 240,000) but the exact number is not known. In Arabic, each prophet is known as a nabi (prophet of Allah); collectively they are known as **anbiya**. Among them are those who received messages directly from God and such a prophet is known as a rasul (messenger). The others were preachers of previous messages.

Four divine books are mentioned in the Qur'an: Tawrah (the Torah), revealed to Musa; Zabur (the Psalms), revealed to Dawud; Injil (the Gospel), revealed to Isa; and Qur'an, revealed to the Prophet Muhammad. Therefore the Prophet Muhammad is seen as the final link in the succession of prophets and he is also seen as the perfect prophet or 'perfect pattern'. This is because he exemplified not only how humans should live but also demonstrated perfect harmony of heart, as described on page 106.

The Prophet Muhammad

It is important for Muslims to study the life of the Prophet Muhammad, found in the Sirah (biographical writings about the life of the Prophet), and his teachings, which are contained in the Hadith (sayings of the Prophet). Also important for Muslims is the Sunnah, the custom and practices of the Prophet Muhammad, which provides practical interpretations of how to apply the guidance of the Qur'an in their daily life. In his last sermon the Prophet Muhammad said:

> I leave behind me two things, the Qur'an and my example the Sunnah, and if you follow these you will never go astray.

The Prophet Muhammad was born in Makkah in 570CE. His father died when he was young and, after the death of his foster mother, he was brought up by his Uncle Abu Talib. Muslims believe that Allah made him experience the sorrows of being an orphan, and the fact that he was poor made sure he knew the sufferings of poverty. As he grew up he was well liked and obtained the name al-Amin (trustworthy). He came to be seen as wise. An example of an event that happened when he was 35 years old illustrates this.

At that time in Makkah the **Ka'bah** (believed to be Adam's shrine to God) was being rebuilt. Conflict arose amongst the different tribes in Makkah as to who would replace the Black Stone. This stone is embedded in the wall of the Ka'bah and today Muslims believe it to be sacred. The different tribes of the city were arguing and the Prophet Muhammad was called in to arbitrate. He spread his cloak, put the Black Stone on it and then asked all the tribal leaders to raise the cloak and take the Stone to the Ka'bah. Muhammad then placed the Stone in its right place. This satisfied the leaders and peace was restored. From childhood he had been a devotee of Allah and had rejected the idol worship that had been characteristic of the Ka'bah. He was dissatisfied with the values of Makkan society, which he judged to be unjust, corrupt, materialistic and cruel. He also worked to help the poor and suffering.

When the Prophet Muhammad was 25 years old a rich widow named Khadijah offered to marry him. This increased his material wealth, but from that time onwards he would go to a cave in Mount Hira, which lies between Makkah and a place called Mina, and spend days and nights in meditation. He did this especially during the month of **Ramadan**. At the age of 40, the Prophet Muhammad received his first revelation from the Angel Jibreel (Gabriel). The angel commanded the Prophet Muhammad to:

> Recite. In the Name of the Lord who created, created Man from a blood-clot. Recite. And the Lord is the Most Generous who taught by the Pen, taught Man, that he knew not.
>
> Surah 96: 1–5

This profound religious experience had a deep effect on the Prophet Muhammad and the next 13 years were spent preaching to the people of Makkah, secretly at first but later on openly, and leading them away from idolatry to the worship of Allah. However, the Makkan establishment didn't accept his message and in 622CE, after the death of his wife, he left Makkah for Madinah.

In Madinah some tribal leaders, who had met Muhammad in Makkah, had embraced Islam, and some of the Prophet Muhammad's followers had already visited Madinah to preach Islam. This migration is called Hijrah (departure), and it is from this date that the Islamic calendar is calculated: the month when this happened, Muharram, became the first month of the calendar. Therefore 622CE became year 1AH (anno Hegirae) for Muslims. Sometimes, Hijrah is translated as 'flight' but this is not correct, as it was a planned migration. The intention was to set up a new capital in order to reclaim the old Makkah. Hijrah also meant the leaving of all home ties for the sake of God.

Almost half of the Prophet Muhammad's years as a prophet of Allah were spent in Madinah. It was also a time when the revelation from Allah widened to include details about prayer, fasting, charity, pilgrimage, and social and economic matters concerned with improving society. In Makkah the revelations were short and were concerned largely with the basic beliefs about Allah and the Day of Judgement.

The revelation of the Qur'an was completed during the Prophet Muhammad's period in Madinah and the revelation was preserved in its purity by huffaz (memorisers, singular hafiz).

Huffaz were people taught by the Prophet Muhammad to memorise the whole of the Qur'an. The first school consequently emerged in connection with the Prophet's Mosque in Madinah.

This period also saw the development of Islamic identity – a brotherly bond established by Muhammad that meant that religious allegiance transcended all family and tribal ties. This is the genesis of a significant characteristic of Islam as a religion for the whole of humanity. Also established at this time was the qibla (direction of prayer). It had previously lain in the direction of Jerusalem and now it was centred on Makkah where, Muslims believe, Adam built the first House of God, modelled on one in heaven – the Ka'bah.

However, relations remained hostile between Makkah and Madinah. Two significant battles were fought at this time. In 624CE, the Battle of Badr saw a small Muslim army defeat a much larger contingent from Makkah. The following year, however, the Muslims lost the Battle of Uhud against a huge Makkan army. In 627CE, Madinah was under siege from the Makkans but the Madinans successfully protected their city by digging a trench around it. The unsuccessful seige ultimately led to a peace treaty that allowed Muslims to visit Makkah on pilgrimage. In 630CE, however, the peace treaty was broken and an army of 20,000 Muslims advanced on Makkah. The city was 'captured' without any bloodshed and the Prophet Muhammad spared the lives of his opponents, insisting only that the idols of the city be destroyed. In 632CE, the Prophet Muhammad went to Makkah on pilgrimage for the last time and in so doing established the rites of the **hajj** (see pages 122–3). In Makkah, he gave his famous farewell sermon that included the principle of universal human rights and the enforcing of the Five Pillars of Islam (see pages 118–23).

Why you need to know these facts

Many religions teach that God's message is mediated through prophets of one sort or another. Teaching along the lines of 'How can people know about God?' is a useful way of learning about the prophets of Islam. Learning about the life of the

Prophet Muhammad is essential because much Muslim practice derives from his own practice, as recorded in the Sunnah. However, it is important to learn not only his biographical details but also about his teachings, the Hadith. There are many useful books derived from the Hadith.

Vocabulary

Anbiya (singular nabi) – prophets; to be distinguished from rasul (messenger).
Ka'bah – the shrine in the Grand Mosque in Makkah, said to have been built by Adam and rebuilt by Ibrahim.
Ramadan – the ninth month of the Muslim calendar; the month of fasting.

Sensitive issues

Because the Prophet Muhammad is regarded as merely a human being, albeit a special one, nobody should draw or paint pictures of him. This, Muslims believe, could lead to idolatry. Note also that Muslims always say 'peace be upon him' after mentioning the name of any prophet.

Common misconceptions

We have already noted it is a common fallacy to assume that the Prophet Muhammad is the founder of Islam. Although Muslims believe that the Prophet Muhammad was a perfect human being they did not believe he was divine in any way. Therefore it is a fallacy to assume that Muslims see the Prophet Muhammad in the same way that Christians see Jesus. The old label for Islam of Muhammadanism is deeply offensive to Muslims as it implies that the Prophet Muhammad is an object of worship; for Muslims, this is shirk, the greatest Muslim sin.

Amazing facts

As we have noted, the Prophet did not write down any of the words of the Qur'an. Islam teaches that God had given him an inexhaustible memory and so he was able to memorise the whole of it. He taught others to do this. A person who memorises the Qur'an is called hafiz.

Teaching ideas

- Explore different ways in which people send and receive messages. Design a poster to illustrate some of these.
- Learn about some of the prophets of Islam, for example Moses and Jesus.
- Read some of the stories, available from the Islamic Foundation, about the practices of the Prophet Muhammad, and explore the spiritual and moral messages of each story.

Sources of Islam

Subject facts

The Qur'an
The Qur'an was revealed to the Prophet Muhammad over a period of 23 years. These revelations were not written down at the time but memorised. The Prophet's close companions jotted down the words of each recitation on any material they had to hand. Some committed the words to memory. The revelations to the Prophet ceased two years before his death, and it is reported that during his last year the Prophet recited the whole of the Qur'an twice. The writings were collected together soon after his death under the direction of his successor, Abu Bakr. Various copies were circulated during these years until the third successor of the Prophet Muhammad, Uthman, collected them together and issued a standardised version.

The Qur'an (recitation) is written in Arabic, the language of the original revelations. Muslims believe that throughout history God has revealed his message to the people in Arabic, even though the message is for everyone. The final and most perfect revelation was in the language of Arabic and, consequently, Muslims do not accept translations of the Qur'an as authentic. A translation would lose the original flavour of the words and their meanings, and so alter the Word of God.

The Qur'an is arranged in surahs (chapters). There are 114 surahs in the Qur'an. These are not arranged in order of revelation but of length – from longest to shortest. This means that, apart from the first surah, **Fatihah** (The Opening), the early surahs that were revealed to the Prophet Muhammad during his time in Makkah are placed at the back of the Qur'an. These early surahs were revealed when the Prophet Muhammad was teaching a simple message of belief in Allah and the Day of Judgement. The later and longer surahs at the front of the Qur'an were revealed in Madinah and contain great detail about guidance for living as a Muslim. Each surah, except one, begins with the words, 'In the name of Allah, the Merciful, the Compassionate. This is called the **Bismillah**, which means 'In the name of Allah' in Arabic.

So important is the Qur'an for Muslims that it is treated in a number of ways that illustrate respect: it may be wrapped in a clean cloth; it will be kept on a high shelf, above other books; many Muslims will wash their hands before touching the Qur'an; it may be placed on a stand when it is being read to make sure it does not touch the floor – the Qur'an should never be in the lowest position; some Muslims will kiss the Qur'an after reading it and may avoid turning their backs to it when they leave the room.

Muslims believe that the Qur'an is the final and most comprehensive book of spiritual knowledge and instructions. Only those who approach reading it with iman (faith) may understand its true meaning. Without faith, the human spirit is prevented from understanding the true meaning of the Qur'an. The Qur'an provides for Muslims a holistic worldview that takes into account everything about this world and the next. It provides instructions as to how Muslims may organise their lives according to the will of Allah. This is, however, a constant **jihad** (struggle) because the forces of the world do their best to distract people from the ways of God and the Prophet Muhammad.

The Hadith

Although the Qur'an is the main source of guidance because it is the Word of God, Muslims also have the Hadith. 'Hadith' means 'statement' or 'report' and refers to reports of what the Prophet Muhammad said and did during his prophethood. Most Muslims accept six books of the Hadith as being authentic and trustworthy. They are named after their collectors and were collected during the first three centuries of Islam. The two most authoritative are called Sahih al-Bukhari and Sahih Muslim. The word 'sahih' means 'authentic'. The authentic Hadith also include a record of the Sunnah of the Prophet Muhammad, the custom and practice of the Prophet. For example, the exact times for **salah** follow the practice of the Prophet and are not given in the Qur'an. The Qur'an states:

You have a good example in God's messenger.

Surah 33: 21

Why you need to know these facts

The Qur'an and Hadith provide guidance for Muslims as to how to live their lives according to God's will. All religions provide guidance for believers and all humans follow some guidance or another in their lives. The topic of guidance opens up all kinds of issues related to our shared human experience and learning about the sources of Islam is best done in the light of this. Using guidance as a theme is much more educationally sound, and truer to the nature of Islam, than merely concentrating on the Qur'an as a special book.

Vocabulary

Fatihah – the opening surah of the Qur'an:

In the name of God, Most Gracious, Most Merciful. Praise be to God, The Cherisher and Sustainer of the Worlds; Most Gracious, Most Merciful; Master of the Day of Judgement.

Jihad – struggle, both physical and moral.

Sensitive issues

Always be very careful how you handle a Qur'an. You should, ideally, wash your hands before touching it, keep it clean by wrapping it in a cloth and keep it in a high position. If displaying the Qur'an, do not leave it open on a Qur'an stand when it is not being read.

Common misconceptions

Due to the common practice in the West of seeing religions as separate systems of belief, many people new to Islam are surprised to find out that the Qur'an includes stories and accounts that can be found in the Bible, albeit with different names and in some cases a different emphasis. It is worth remembering that although the Qur'an is, according to Muslim belief, the final and most perfect revelation, it is not completely separate from the revelations, albeit distorted revelations, contained in sacred scripture such as the Bible.

Teaching ideas

● Show the children copies of the Qur'an in Arabic and copies translated into English. Ask the children what differences they can see between the copies.
● Read together and get the children to copy out some key surahs, for example Surah 1 and Surah 96. Get the children to illustrate their surahs after looking at highly decorated versions of the Qur'an.
● Discuss with the children the idea of guidance. From whom or where do they get their guidance? What sort of guidance is important for them? Do we all need guidance? As a class, look at the ways in which the Qur'an is a guide for Muslims.
● If possible, visit a madrasah and find out about what the children learn there.

The Five Pillars

Subject facts

The Five Pillars of Islam come under the heading of worship or 'belief in action', called **ibadah**. They are the duties that support the whole way of life for a Muslim. It is said that, in Islam, faith and practice are a seamless robe. In practising the Five Pillars, Muslims obey Allah and follow the practice of the Prophet Muhammad. The Five Pillars enable Muslims to realise their true self, to develop personal characteristics and become the kind of people that Allah wants them to be. This is only true, of course, if the rituals are performed with sincerity and **niyyah** (the right intention).

The Five Pillars of Islam

1. The Shahadah – Muslims should recite the Shahadah.
2. Salah – Muslims should pray five times a day.
3. Zakah – Muslims should give zakah.
4. Sawm – Muslims should fast during Ramadan.
5. Hajj – Muslims should go on a pilgrimage to Makkah.

First Pillar: the Shahadah

The first duty of a Muslim is to recite the Shahadah, the declaration of faith, as often as possible. It underpins everything that a Muslim does. It expresses his or her intention to turn his or her whole life towards Allah. It declares his or her belief in the Prophet Muhammad as the final messenger of Allah and his or her intention to follow the Sunnah (the path and example of the Prophet) as closely as possible.

I bear witness that there is no god but Allah and I bear witness that the Prophet Muhammad is His messenger.

Second Pillar: Salah

The second duty of a Muslim is to perform salah, the five set daily prayers. These take place at early morning just before sunrise (fajr), at midday (zuhr), in the afternoon (asr), in the evening just after sunset (maghrib) and during the night but before midnight (isha). It says in the Qur'an:

> Preserve prayer and especially the middle prayer.
> Surah 2: 238

There are different interpretations for what 'the middle prayer' means. Perhaps the most significant one says it refers to the prayer of the heart (qalb). In other words, the heart must be engaged when praying – prayer must not become merely a ritual, mechanical exercise. The Prophet Muhammad said that unless the heart is engaged, and the person's intention right, the prayer is unacceptable to Allah.

Wudu

To ensure that this intention is right, a Muslim has a duty to prepare properly for prayer and to perform the ablutions of purification called **wudu**. Islamic practice is all about internal change through outward action. Parts of the body are washed in a set way:

- First, Muslims wash their hands up to the wrist three times and ask God to cleanse them of any sins they may have committed by deed or word, either knowingly or unknowingly.
- Next, Muslims clean their nostrils three times and pray to God that they may be pure enough to smell the sweetness of Paradise.
- Then they wash their face three times and ask that their face may display the light of God.
- Next, Muslims wash both their arms and ask God that they may be placed with the righteous on the Day of Judgement and not with the sinners.
- Then they pass the palm of their hand over their head, starting from the top of the forehead to the back and then pass both hands over the back of their neck – this is a prayer for mercy so that suffering may not 'hang around the neck'.
- Next, Muslims rinse their ears so that they may grow pure in character and only hear what is good.

● Finally, they wash both their feet – the right for righteousness and the left to pray to God that they may be saved from the lure of the path to hell.

They are now ready to offer salah.

Rak'ah

Each of the prayers has a fixed set of actions called **rak'ah**. First, men raise their hands to their ears and women raise their hands to their shoulders. Secondly, men and women fold their hands in front of them. Thirdly, they bow. Fourthly, they stand upright again and then, finally, they prostrate themselves. In this way, the rak'ah illustrates the gradual submission to Allah. After a Muslim has completed this first rak'ah, he or she sits back before performing another series of the same actions.

Each prayer stipulates a different number of these rak'ahs. For fajr there are two, for zuhr four, for asr four, for maghrib three, and for isha four. As well as performing these actions, a Muslim recites praise for Allah and quotations from the Qur'an. When the correct number of rak'ahs are complete, the worshipper turns his or her head to the right and then to the left whilst saying the words 'assalamu alaikum', which invokes God's blessing and peace upon all those people to the right and all those to the left. On Friday there is a congregational prayer (see page 132).

Third Pillar: Zakah

The third pillar is **zakah**, which means the purification of wealth by obligatory giving to the community. Very often this is paid at the end of Ramadan along with **sadaqat ul-fitr**. It is recognition of the fact that all good things are a gift from Allah. It also teaches Muslims to accept responsibility for supporting the ummah (the Muslim community) and people in need. Many Muslims call zakah the 'poor due' because all have a duty to give it and the poor have a right to receive it. It is calculated at 2.5 per cent of a person's disposable income. Those who have no surplus money do not have to pay it.

In some Islamic countries it operates like a tax and is collected by the government. In Britain, Muslims often send the money to developing countries, such as Bangladesh or India. This illustrates the Muslim sense of identity and obligation to the worldwide ummah. As well as helping others, zakah also purifies the giver of selfishness and greed. It is a statement of the need for a fairer society and the duty to break down divisions between rich and poor.

Fourth Pillar: Sawm

The Prophet Muhammad fasted during the lunar month of Ramadan. It was during this time that he received the first revelation of the Qur'an. Fasting (**sawm**) during Ramadan is obligatory for all adult Muslims, except for pregnant or menstruating women, Muslims with illness, those travelling and elderly Muslims. These people should either fast later, or help feed the poor if they are unable to fast. Children under 12 do not have to fast, but many children younger than 12 may begin to practise fasting by giving things up for short periods. Those fasting should not eat, drink, smoke or have sexual intercourse between dawn and sunset.

The fast is broken each day at sunset with a light meal (**iftar**) beginning with a glass of water and some dates. There are several reasons for fasting. It helps Muslims develop the characteristics of God who has no physical needs to satisfy. It trains them to identify with those who suffer hunger and thirst in the world. Very importantly, however, it exercises a Muslim's control over his or her physical desires. This is essential if the person is to achieve the harmony of heart exemplified by the Prophet Muhammad. Again, internal change is the purpose of fasting. So it is no good in the eyes of Allah to merely refrain from eating and drinking if the person behaves unkindly to others or thinks ill of anybody.

One night during Ramadan is especially important. This is known as the 'Night of Power'. Most Muslims observe this day on the 27th day of the month and remember the revelation of the Qur'an to the Prophet Muhammad. For this day, some Muslims separate themselves from the rest of the community and go into retreat; this is called **I'tikaf** and involves study of the Qur'an. A part of the mosque may be separated off with white sheets hung up like curtains to enable people to devote themselves to this study.

Ramadan ends with the festival of **Id ul-Fitr**. It is a period of happiness and thanksgiving after the long month of fasting. It begins when the full moon is visible at the end of the month. Muslims will wear best or new clothes and celebrate together as a family and visit relatives. All Muslims will break the fast by giving charity to those in need. This is called sadaqat ul-fitr. In this country Id ul-Fitr is increasingly seen as a holiday when people may take a day or two off work or school.

Fifth Pillar: Hajj

It is an obligation for all Muslims to undertake the hajj (the annual pilgrimage to Makkah) at least once in their lifetime, if they are fit and able. Not every Muslim manages to achieve this because to go on the hajj a Muslim must fulfil certain criteria. Firstly, he or she should be a responsible adult; secondly, he or she should be able to afford it without leaving the family in debt – the hajj can cost thousands of pounds; finally, he or she should be physically fit enough to withstand the rigours of a visit that can take up to two weeks. Men who have performed hajj are referred to as hajji and women as hajja. They feel that performing hajj is a great privilege and are held in respect by the rest of the community. The hajj strengthens a person's faith and enables them to better carry out obedience to Allah.

The hajj itself lasts five or six days and takes place in the month of Dhul-Hijjah, the twelfth month of the Islamic calendar. The Prophet Muhammad set out the actual practices when he performed his only hajj towards the end of his life. There are various ceremonies that take place over the time of the pilgrimage. Seven of the most important are:

● *Each person must put on ihram.* For men, ihram consists of wearing two pieces of white cloth; women usually wear a long white dress with a white headscarf. This is a sign of purity and equality. When everyone wears the same simple clothes, no distinctions between rich and poor can be made. This teaches Muslims that everyone is equal in the sight of Allah. Pilgrims in ihram cannot have sexual relations, kill animals or insects or remove hair from their bodies.

● *Performing tawaf.* Tawaf involves circling the holy Ka'bah seven times and kissing the Black Stone (see page 110). It is not always possible to kiss the Black Stone because the crowds are so large. If kissing is impossible, the Stone should be saluted. Circling the Ka'bah symbolises the unity of Muslims as believers in, and worshippers of, Allah. It also expresses the Muslim belief that the Ka'bah was the very first place built on earth to worship Allah.

● *Running, or walking quickly, between As-Safa and Al-Marwah.*
By joining in this ceremony Muslims remember Hagar and her
concern for her son Ishmail when they were left in the desert
without any water. The story in the Qur'an tells how, in a
desperate search for water, Ishmail dug his heels into the sand
and a spring of water gushed forth. The well that remains is called
the Well of **Zamzam**. Pilgrims may bathe in it or drink from it and
also take some of this life-giving water home with them. It reminds
the pilgrims that Allah looks after all who are obedient to Him.

● *Visiting Arafat.* The most important aspect of the hajj. Pilgrims
stand before Allah on the Mount of Mercy and beg forgiveness
for their sins. The Plain of Arafat lies 24km east of Makkah.

● *Stoning the Devil at Mina.* The pilgrims collect pebbles from
the Plain of Arafat and when they arrive at Mina they throw
seven stones at each of three stone pillars. These pillars represent
the devil (**Shaytan**) and recall the story of Ibrahim and his son
Ishmail, when Allah tested Ibrahim's faith by demanding the
sacrifice of his son. The devil tempted Ibrahim to resist doing it
three times, hence the three pillars. Both father and son resisted
the temptation to disobey Allah by throwing stones at the devil.
By throwing the stones, the pilgrims not only remember the
story and example of Ibrahim, but also make a resolve to resist
temptation and evil in their own lives.

● *Many Muslim men cut their hair at the end of the hajj.* It is an
expression of closeness to Allah and the belief that all outward
appearances should give way to complete devotion and
submission to Allah.

● *Many pilgrims offer a sacrifice of an animal,* usually a sheep or
goat, if they can afford it. This takes place at Mina on the tenth
day of the month. It recalls Ibrahim eventually sacrificing a ram
instead of his son. This sacrifice reminds pilgrims that they must
give up everything for Allah. Whilst pilgrims are carrying out this
sacrifice, Muslims all over the world celebrate the festival of Id
ul-Adha (a major festival, sometimes called Big Id). The festival,
in which Muslims give to charity, has the same meaning as the
sacrifice performed by the pilgrims in Makkah. Like Id ul-Fitr, this is
a holiday and time for special prayers and family celebrations.

Why you need to know these facts

A study of the Five Pillars not only enables children to learn about how Muslims express their beliefs, but also offers an opportunity for children to reflect on what duties and routines in their own lives help give their life meaning. The idea of a pillar that holds up buildings can be explored along with what, for example, gives our own lives solidity and support. The idea of regular duties and discipline is another aspect of this topic that can be related to children's own lives.

Vocabulary

Hajj – pilgrimage to Makkah; a male who has performed the hajj is called hajji, and a female hajja.

Ibadah – worship.

Id ul-Fitr – festival that breaks the fast of Ramadan, beginning a day after Ramadan ends. It is also the first day of Shawal, the tenth Islamic month.

Iftar – breaking of the fast each day during Ramadan.

Ihram – the state entered into when performing hajj or umrah (pilgrimage to Makkah at any time during the year). It also refers to the two pieces of white cloth worn by males and the white, modest clothing worn by females.

I'tikaf – special study of the Qur'an during Ramadan.

Niyyah – right intention.

Rak'ah – fixed set of actions performed during salah.

Sadaqat ul-fitr – voluntary charitable payment.

Salah – the five set, daily prayers.

Sawm – fasting.

Shaytan – rebellious or proud; the devil.

Tawaf – walking seven times around the Ka'bah in worship of Allah.

Wudu – ritual purification; ablutions performed before salah.

Zakah – purification by wealth; an obligatory act of worship in which a devotee gives money to charity.

Zamzam – the well next to the Ka'bah; the place where, according to Muslim belief, water sprang forth for Hagar in answer to her prayers.

Common misconceptions

Those with little empathy for Islam sometimes view the Five
Pillars as being a rather joyless, over-disciplined way of life. However,
the keeping of the Five Pillars is not merely outwardly ritualistic –
that would make them useless in the eyes of God – but must
involve sincere intention of the heart. In this sense the practice of
Muslims is a joyful and spiritually enriching way to live one's life.

Amazing facts

Each year, around 2 million people make the pilgrimage to
Makkah. There have been a number of tragedies including, in
1990, the crushing to death of nearly 1500 pilgrims in a tunnel
leading to the holy sites. More recently, in 2006, a stampede killed
over 300 and injured 289 more.

Teaching ideas

- Discuss with the children the things they do regularly each day
at home and at school. Ask them why they do these things.
- Look at artefacts connected with prayer, for example the
compass and prayer mat. Find the direction of Makkah and mark
it on the wall. Display the children's work on Islam in that area.
- Copy out and illustrate the call to prayer.
- Invent a short fast in class and rules to go with it.
- Write out some surahs from the Qur'an that refer to
Ramadan and decorate them with Islamic patterns or calligraphy.
- Write an acrostic poem based on words such as Ramadan,
fasting, self-discipline.
- Find out about Muslim organisations, such as Islamic Relief, and
the causes they support. Decide together on a cause or charity
to which the class can give. Ask the children to design some rules
for giving, such as what, when and how much to give.
- Discuss with the children what people should spend money
on to make the world a better place.

- Discuss the idea, with examples from the children, of a special journey.
- Get each child to design a brochure for the hajj that describes and explains the rituals. This could also be linked to a geography lesson on where Makkah is.

Family life and life rituals

Subject facts

Worship at home

Religious life for most Muslims is very much centred on the home. Many Muslims take off their shoes when entering the house, and visitors will be asked to do the same. This is because, in a very real sense, the house is a mosque as well as a home. The Qur'an may be prominently displayed on a high shelf somewhere in the house, and one room will be kept especially clean for the regular saying of salah. In this room a quotation from the Qur'an, or a suitable sign, may be placed on the wall to mark the direction of Makkah. Prayer mats will be placed on the floor and the father will usually lead the prayers. Other members of the family arrange themselves in lines behind the person who is leading the prayers. Many Muslim families offer prayers before and after meals. They will say Bismillah before and **Alhamdulillah** after.

Food and drink

Muslims have strict rules about food and drink. Foods are either declared halal, allowed, or haram, forbidden. Haram food includes pigs, animals that eat other animals, animals or birds that have died naturally or from disease, animals strangled to death, animals slaughtered in the incorrect way and animals' blood. For meat to be halal, the animal should be killed with a sharp knife and the blood should flow freely. Jewish **kosher** meat is halal for Muslims. Muslims also do not drink alcohol or take any other intoxicants.

Children's upbringing

The home is where children learn the Muslim way of life. They are taught to be respectful, especially to their parents. The Prophet

Muhammad taught that all are born Muslim. It is the parents who determine whether or not a child grows up to be a Muslim, a Christian or a Jew and so on. There are various ceremonies that are designed to ensure that children grow up to be good Muslims.

The adhan and 'aqiqah
The birth of a child is regarded as a blessing from God, and as soon as the child is born the father recites the **adhan** in the baby's right ear and the **aqamah** into the left. This is to cement the name of God and the call to prayer into the child's brain. Seven days after the birth, the child is named in a ceremony called 'aqiqah. A goat or sheep is sacrificed for a daughter or two goats or sheep for a son. A third of the meat is given to the needy, a third to relatives and neighbours, and a third is eaten by the family. In some countries, something sweet is put on the baby's lips to symbolise the hope that the child will grow up to be pleased to be a Muslim. Some parents arrange for the baby's hair to be cut off soon after birth. For male children circumcision is a **Sunnah**. Nowadays, this is carried out in hospital.

Bismillah ceremony
A Muslim child learns about religious practice and reading the Qur'an at home. By the time the child reaches the age of four or five there is a Bismillah ceremony to initiate the child into reciting the opening surah (chapter) of the Qur'an and writing the first few letters of the Arabic alphabet. The child is given new clothes and a pious relative, or an alim (learned man), makes the child repeat with him the Surah Fatihah and the first few lines of Surah 96 – the first revelation to the Prophet Muhammad, which begins with the word 'iqra' (recite or read).

Marriage
Muslims believe that Allah intends that people should live together as families. Consequently, marriage is taken very seriously. While according to Muslim law both partners should give their free consent to marriage, there are rules about the involvement of the family, which include making sure that the couple are compatible. For Muslims, a marriage is not just the joining together of two individuals but the coming together of two families. Generally, Muslim women cannot marry men who are not Muslims, although

a Muslim man may marry a woman who is a practising Christian or Jew, but the woman should not be forced to become a Muslim.

For women, their main responsibility is to look after and care for the family. She should not have more than one husband. A man must give a dowry to the woman he is marrying. In special cases, and if the law of the country allows, a man may have up to four wives, as long as he treats them all the same.

Ceremonies associated with marriage vary according to cultural tradition. Often, the couple receive gifts from relatives and friends. The wedding may be held at home or in a mosque. The groom may lead his family to the bride's house. The men meet in one room and the women in another. It is usually the **imam** at the mosque who conducts the marriage ceremony. He first asks the woman if she is willing to marry the man. Sometimes this is asked three times. The imam then calls on the man to recite some words from the Qur'an, and asks him if he is willing to marry the woman. The imam then declares the couple married and a marriage contract is signed.

Death

Muslims believe in life after death and the Day of Judgement, when everyone will be asked to account for his or her life on Earth. Accordingly, someone will recite the Shahadah (see page 105) into the ear of the dying person. This, Muslims believe, will help the person answer correctly what they believe. The dying person may be placed so that he or she is facing Makkah and therefore looking in the direction of the Ka'bah (see page 113). When the person has died, friends and relatives will visit the family to comfort them. They will pray and read from the Qur'an.

The Prophet Muhammad gave detailed descriptions about what should happen to the body of a dead person. It should be washed ritually at least three times. This must start at the right side of the body and follow the rituals of wudu – the person is being prepared for his or her last prayer. Perfume is often placed in the body's hair and the parts of the body used in prayer – the hands, feet, knees and forehead. After it is washed, the body is wrapped in a special white shroud.

If a person has been on hajj, he or she will be dressed in ihram (see page 122). Depending on when a person dies, the body may be taken to the mosque on a Friday for the person's last jum'a prayer (see page 132). Muslims bury their dead because they believe in physical resurrection. At the graveside, the imam will say a special prayer and the following words are recited from the Qur'an:

> We have created you from this earth and We shall
> return you into it and then shall bring you forth out
> of it once again.
>
> Surah 20: 55

The body is then placed on its side in the grave, facing Makkah. Muslim graves are simple with simple headstones. Muslims believe all people are equal in the sight of God and so ornate headstones are discouraged.

Why you need to know these facts

The growth of a person from life to death takes place for a Muslim within the context of the ummah (community). The family is a microcosm of the worldwide Muslim ummah – it is a community within a community. This idea that we are individuals but also part of a greater whole is central to Muslim belief and provides opportunities for children to explore ideas about identity and meaning for human beings. This should be kept in mind when teaching about life rituals in Islam.

Vocabulary

Adhan – the call to prayer.
Alhamdulillah – 'All praise be to Allah.'
Aqamah – the call to begin prayer.
Bismillah al Rahman al Rahim – 'In the name of God, the Merciful, the Compassionate'; the preface to all surahs of the Qur'an except the ninth.
Imam – leader of congregational prayers.
Kosher – 'proper'; describes food fit to eat according to Jewish dietary laws.
Sunnah – a tradition or custom founded on the example of the Prophet Muhammad.

Sensitive issues

Nudity is strictly forbidden in Islam except for medical reasons. For example, a Muslim pupil will not be allowed to have a shower with his or her classmates without underwear.

Common misconceptions

- There are so many potential misunderstandings connected with how Muslims live their lives. The role of women in the family is one such area. Many in the West perceive Muslim women to be downtrodden. This is not necessarily the case. Many aspects of Muslim practice are cultural rather than religious; for example the Qur'an commands that men and women be modest in their manner of dress and different Muslims interpret how a woman should dress according to cultural tradition. Strictly speaking, women should cover the head, arms and feet and not take off outer garments in the presence of males unrelated to them. Not all Muslim women will interpret this as wearing full black veils and black robes; some Muslim women in Britain will wear a modest style of Western dress and no veil. However, the idea of the woman having her most important role in the home is truly Islamic. The value of nurturing the family is the most important thing a person can do. That is why the Prophet Muhammad is reported as saying that 'Paradise lies at the feet of your mother.' Furthermore, the view that God created men as superior to women is not true. The Qur'an says that both were created with equal but different responsibilities.
- In the context of RE, Muslim life rituals, such as the adhan and the 'aqiqah' are often misunderstood in the context of initiation. What they represent is initiation into the Muslim way of life. They do not correspond to other religion's rituals, such as Christian baptism. The two religions do not share the same views about human nature. To become a Christian requires the washing away of sin. This idea does not feature in Muslim belief.

> ## Teaching ideas

● Discuss with the children what makes a house a home. Make lists of the characteristics and differences of each.
● Learn about the variety of practices in a Muslim home. Get the children to illustrate them and write down what belief is being expressed by each.
● Discuss how babies are looked after and why they are so special. Discuss what babies can do for themselves and what adults can do for them.
● Discuss what the children have learnt from their parents and teachers about how to live a good life.
● Discuss why people get married and look at some of the rules for Muslim marriage. Look at a Muslim marriage contract and get the children to think what they might put in their own contract and design one.
● Design an information sheet for non-Muslims about how Muslims treat a person when they are dying. Discuss with the children their own ideas about life after death.
● Find sections in the Qur'an that describe Paradise, for example Surahs 13: 35, 47: 15, 39: 71–75. Get the children to do some imaginative writing about heaven.

Ummah

> ## Subject facts

As we have noted, Islam is a multi-cultural world religion. The ummah (community) is a great unifying force – all Muslims, whether they are black, white, Asian and so on, are not only citizens of their own country but members of the Muslim ummah. The ummah is described in the Qur'an:

> *Now you are the best community which has been raised up for the guidance of mankind; you enjoin what is right and forbid what is wrong and believe in Allah.*
>
> Surah 3

Prayer and worship in the mosque

For most Muslims the centre of their local community is the mosque – a focal point for social and communal activities – but most of all it is a place of prayer. The Arabic word for mosque is *masjid*, which means 'place of prostration'.

In a mosque, Muslims are called to prayer with the words of the adhan, performed by the **muezzin**, who faces Makkah, in some cases from the top of a tower called a minaret. In Britain, the muezzin performs the adhan from inside the mosque and it is sometimes broadcast through a speaker from the minaret. Of course many mosques in the UK are converted buildings so do not have a minaret.

On Friday there is a special prayer said in the mosque, called the jum'a prayer. This prayer is in fact the zuhr prayer (see page 119) but it is special because on a Friday it is performed as a congregational prayer. Friday is not a holy day as such but all Muslim men should leave their worldly activities and attend the mosque for this prayer. Women do not have to attend the mosque as they have domestic duties that in Islamic thinking are considered highly important. The service in the mosque usually begins just after midday and lasts for about an hour and a half, although the actual prayer only lasts for about ten minutes. Some Muslim men will attend the mosque for a brief period of time whilst others will arrive early and perform their own, personal, prayers, called du'a.

Before the jum'a prayer there will be a sermon called the khutbah. This is given by the imam and lasts about 20 minutes. It is usually a speech that explains various passages from the Qur'an, or aspects of the life of the Prophet Muhammad and their significance and meaning for Muslims today. In larger mosques, the khutbah may be delivered in a common language such as Urdu and, increasingly, an English translation will follow. After a second call to prayer called the iqamah, which warns everybody that the prayer is about to start, the worshippers will all stand shoulder to shoulder to perform the rak'ahs. In large mosques in cities like London, Bradford or Birmingham, as many as 3000 people may attend the jum'a prayer on a Friday. Others will pray in smaller mosques, but if we remember that Birmingham alone has more than 100 mosques, some

admittedly very small, that means a lot of people at prayer!
After the prayer, most people will leave and resume their daily
activities. Others may remain to socialise or read the Qur'an.

Features of a mosque

Purpose-built mosques have a dome, a minaret for the call to
prayer and a prayer hall with a qibla wall – a wall that faces
Makkah and towards which everyone offers their prayers.
Within the qibla is a small recess called a mihrab. This points
worshippers in the right direction for prayer and provides
amplification for the imam when leading the prayers. The only
piece of furniture in the prayer hall is a minbar – a platform,
usually with three steps, from which the imam preaches the
khutbah on a Friday. All prayer halls are carpeted. Muslims also
use a prayer mat as it is important that prayer is said from a
clean place. Everyone removes his or her shoes before entering
the prayer hall. Women cover their bodies and heads, and men,
whilst not having to cover their heads, often do so out of respect.
Large mosques usually have a separate area for women to
worship. Separate from the prayer hall are the washing facilities
where people can perform wudu (see pages 119–20).

In larger mosques there are other rooms for meetings and
educational purposes. Most mosques provide education for
young people in the madrasah. Children attend the madrasah
from as early as five or six years old until their mid-teens.
Classes usually take place each day after school, between five
and seven o'clock. The children study the Qur'an, Islamic studies
(which includes the history of Islam and the life of the Prophet)
and in many cases a community or family language such as Urdu.
Children will also take lessons in Arabic, which is essential for
them to be able to read the Qur'an. Some children learn to
become a hafiz (memoriser of the Qur'an).

Some large mosques have a mortuary attached to them.
This provides a place for a Muslim's body to be prepared for
burial in the correct way (see pages 128–9). Some large mosques
may also house a library and provide adult study facilities.
Mosques also act as centres for welfare organisations and some
engage in inter-faith dialogue.

Why you need to know these facts

As already noted in the section on family life, on page 129, Muslims, whatever their cultural background, identify themselves as part of the worldwide brotherhood of Islam. The idea of belonging to a local community centred on a place of worship is common to many religions and helps reinforce that religious identity for believers. This could be a common theme for study, as well as learning about how the activities at the mosque help Muslims live out their lives according to the will of Allah.

Vocabulary

Muezzin – a man who calls Muslims to prayer.
Shi'a or **Shi'ites** – members of a branch of Islam that separated from the orthodox Sunnis in 679CE due to differences about the succession after the death of the Prophet Muhammad. They constitute about 15 per cent of the world's Islamic population.

Sensitive issues

A number of things need to be remembered when visiting a mosque. Firstly, girls and women should cover their heads and bodies; boys and men do not have to cover their heads but many choose to do so out of respect. When sitting in the prayer hall, do not allow the children to point their feet towards the qiblah wall, nor at other people in the hall.

Common misconceptions

There is sometimes confusion about the role of the imam in Islam. In fact the word is used in three different ways.

First, an imam is a leader of the prayers in a local community. He is knowledgeable in the Qur'an, but he is not ordained – the majority of Muslims who belong to the Sunni tradition believe that all people are equal in the sight of God. Second, 'imam' can refer to great scholars within the different 'schools' of Islamic law.

Third, for **Shi'a** Muslims, the imam acts as an intercessor with authority and spiritual knowledge. They believe that God has designated a line of leaders from the time of Ali (the Prophet's son-in-law). The largest Shi'a group, often called 'Twelvers', believe there can be no more than 12 imams and that the last of these is 'hidden' but will emerge to begin a time of peace. Until that time, certain individuals are singled out as having special authority and are known as maraji'-I taqlid (Centres of Imitation). All believers are expected to defer to this figure in terms of religious judgement. In Iran, the term Ayatollah (literally 'a sign of Allah') is used to signify such a figure.

Amazing facts

The Regent's Park Mosque in London is looked after by a body of people comprising representatives of nearly every Muslim country in the world.

Teaching ideas

- If possible, visit a mosque, preferably at prayer time. Arrange for someone to talk to the children about the work of the mosque.
- Design a visitor's guide to a mosque, including information on sensitivities.
- Discuss with the children the idea of community and why it is important for people. Ask them to write an acrostic poem based on the word community. Identify the key points that make community important for Muslims.
- Ask the children to investigate the three most important mosques for Muslims: those in Makkah, Madinah and Jerusalem.

The Islamic personality

Subject facts

Spirituality

In Islam the word for spirituality is **ihsan**. In one Hadith the Prophet Muhammad said of ihsan that:

> It means you should worship God as though you saw Him. If you cannot do so, then always remember He sees you though you do not see Him.

Ihsan therefore is the spiritual awareness of the presence of God. The practices so far described in this chapter are ways of guiding Muslims to this realisation. Many Muslims, particularly those who see life as an inward journey of the spirit, engage in practices that help them grow inwardly. This inward path, or tariqah, is the path of the Sufi. Sufis spend long hours in prayer and devotion and meditate on the 99 names of God with the aid of prayer beads called **subhah**. Such a process is designed to create within the person feelings of peace and gentleness. For a Sufi, this cultivation of inwardness is vital for spiritual development. It ensures the appropriate intention when, for example, praying, fasting or going on hajj. The goal of Sufi practice for many is fana, which means self-noughting. It is the extinguishing of the ego so that the person may become full of the characteristics of God.

Qualities

For Muslims in general the result of obedience to Allah and following the path of the Prophet is a set of dispositions, characteristics and values which make up the 'Islamic personality'. By growing closer to God a person is changed and certain qualities of a person become evident. These include patience, humility, generosity, truthfulness, justice, sincerity, mercy, kindness, hospitality, forgiveness, brotherliness, modesty, trust in Allah, love of Allah, hope in Allah, God fearing, and striving for Allah (or jihad). Developing such qualities enables Muslims to become truly human and realise the absolute and substantial self, which is what God intended for all human beings.

Why you need to know these facts

Learning about Muslim values and the idea of an Islamic personality is an essential element in understanding Islam. If religious education is to be truly meaningful then children, even quite young ones, should be introduced to the spirituality of a tradition. Learning about the spiritual values of Islam helps children understand the point and purpose of the beliefs and practices of the religion.

Vocabulary

Ihsan – spirituality.
Subhah – prayer beads used to count recitations of the names of God.
Tariqah – the 'inward' path of Muslim spirituality, leading to fana or 'self-noughting'. Traditionally an aspect of the Sufi or mystical tradition.

Common misconceptions

Muslims are often portrayed as political fanatics wanting to wage war on the West. While many Muslims have concerns about the materialistic, consumer culture of the West, the picture painted by the media is very misleading and could be seen as Islamophobia. A lot of this misunderstanding revolves around the concept of jihad. Many Westerners translate this term as meaning 'holy war'. In fact it is a spiritual concept meaning internal struggle. This means striving for Allah by struggling with our weaker and baser nature. Only in extreme cases should struggle for Islam be seen in physical terms.

Teaching ideas

- Discuss with the children what makes a good person.
- Get the children to write about a good person they know, making sure to list clearly the person's good characteristics.
- Design a poster that displays the characteristics of a good Muslim. Get the children to design a badge for themselves that illustrates some Muslim characteristics that they would like to have themselves.

Resources

Artefacts suppliers
Religion in Evidence (see page 33 for details).
Articles of Faith (see page 33 for details).

TV programmes
Channel 4 *Animated World Faiths* series for ages 7–11.
Channel 4 *Stop, Look, Listen*, 'Water, Moon, Candle, Tree and Sword'. Suitable for KS1 children.

Useful books
Religion in Focus: Islam by Geoff Teece (Franklin Watts, 2008).
Create and Display: Festivals by Claire Tinker (Scholastic, 2010).
Create and Display: Art and Culture by Claire Tinker (Scholastic, 2011).

Useful websites
www.zpub.com/aaa/zakat.html
www.bbc.co.uk/schools/religion/islam
www.reonline.org.uk
http://retoday.org.uk

Judaism

Chapter 5

The origins of Judaism are recorded in the Tenakh (the Hebrew
Bible) which tells how God entered into a **covenant** (agreement)
with the Patriarch, Abraham, and later with Moses on Mount
Sinai. Hence the Jews are often referred to as 'the chosen
people'. This means they have a great responsibility to live out
God's mitzvot (commandments) for the benefit of the world and
humankind in general.

The Jewish religion is thousands of years old and, in that time,
Jews have lived in many parts of the world. In the earliest times,
Jewish people were known as Israelites (named after the Biblical
figure of Jacob who was also named Israel); they were also called
Hebrews, which was the name given to a nomadic people of
whom the Jews were a part. To be Jewish means to belong to
this group of people who trace their ancestry back to these early
Biblical times.

Traditionally, anyone born of a Jewish mother is Jewish,
whether they are religious or not. This accounts for the term
'secular Jew'. Secular Jews are people who do not follow the
religious rules and practices of Judaism. In more recent times,
some people regard themselves as Jews if only their father is
Jewish. Non-Jews have also converted to Judaism.

Most Jews, regardless of their religious outlook, have in
common a great sense of identity with the Jewish people.
There are several aspects to this. First, Jews share a common
history which stretches right from the Old Testament, through
the foundation of the State of Israel in 1948, to the present day.
Second, Jews share a language. Although many Jews will have
another language as their first tongue, Hebrew is common to
all Jews as the language of prayer, study and education. Third,
Jews are united by a history of persecution. Despite times
of peace and prosperity the history of the Jewish people is

blighted with a litany of discrimination and suffering, the most recent and horrifying example being the Holocaust during World War II.

There is, as in all religious traditions, considerable diversity within Judaism. This diversity comes in two forms: geographical and ideological.

There have been Jewish communities in many parts of the world since the destruction of the first temple in 586BCE. Today, the two major geographical groupings are Sefardi and Ashkenazi Jews. The groupings take their names from the Hebrew names for countries in the Bible which, in later tradition, came to be applied to Spain and Germany respectively. The differences between Sefardi and Ashkenazi Jews are to do with customs rather than ideology. The Sefardi Jews follow Eastern European Jewish customs, and the Ashkenazi Jews follow the customs of Northern, Eastern and Central Europe.

Second, there is ideological diversity, and these ideological differences are more complex and significant in religious terms. The major distinction is between Orthodox Judaism, which in essence is fundamentalist in that it accepts the divine nature of revelation in the Bible and the authority of the rabbinical interpretations, and Reform Judaism, which does not accept the text of the Bible as it now stands as direct revelation from God. Reformed Judaism (which for the purposes of this book includes Progressive and Liberal Jews) began in Germany in the 19th century because some Jews believed that Judaism should become more modern and respond to ideas developing in the modern world. Nevertheless, despite the desire to see Judaism become more modern, Reform Jews did not want to lose their particular Jewish identity.

There are about 275,000 Jews in the UK and, although Judaism has the oldest presence in this country of any non-Christian religion, the population has been decreasing since at least the 1970s. There is a large Jewish community in London, with significant communities in Leeds, Manchester and Glasgow. The majority of Jews in the UK belong to Orthodox synagogues.

In this chapter, the beliefs and practices of Judaism will be described in Orthodox terms with reference to differences in the Reform tradition.

God

Subject facts

Jewish beliefs about God

The prayer that Jews say most often is:

Hear O Israel! The Lord our God, the Lord is One. You shall love the Lord your God with all your heart, with all your spirit and with all your strength.

This is taken from the book of Deuteronomy in the Tenakh and is called the Shema. In many ways it sums up Jewish belief about the oneness of God and the requirement that humanity should love God. Jews believe that God is the creator and sustainer of the universe. Everything that exists or happens in the world depends on God. God is also transcendent, wholly beyond human limitations. This is the paradoxical nature of God, for while God is beyond the world – 'the whole of the earth is full of God's glory' (Isaiah 6:3) – God is also present for human beings as a loving, personal deity. Although God is beyond time, God is fully involved in human history and destiny.

Proof of God's existence

For Jews, there are two significant proofs of the existence of God. Firstly, there is creation itself, the beauty and pattern of nature. A prayer for the morning service says:

Blessed are You, Lord our God, King of the Universe, who forms light and creates darkness, who makes peace and creates all things… How innumerable are Your deeds, O Lord; You have made them all in wisdom. The whole earth is full of Your creations.

Secondly, as shown in the **Torah** (part of the Tenakh), God has been involved with humanity since the moment humans were created. This is most clearly seen in the various covenants made between God and the Jewish people. The first covenant was with Noah and marked an agreement between God and Noah on behalf of all humanity. Jews are required to keep the commandments that were revealed to Moses on Mount Sinai, but even those who are not Jews are required to keep the seven commandments that were revealed to Noah, known as the **Noahide Code**. There were also covenants with Abraham, Isaac and Jacob, and these mark the beginning of God's relationship with the Jewish people.

God and human suffering

God has promised to bless the Jewish people and maintain a close relationship with them forever. Jews believe this regardless of their long history of suffering. The story of Job, a good man who suffers terribly, is told in the Tenakh. Job's suffering leads him to challenge God as to why such suffering should happen to him. God replies, 'Where were you at the foundation of the world?' This suggests that human perception is too limited to understand how suffering fits into the pattern of things. Therefore the only response for Jews is to put their faith and trust in God.

Nevertheless, the question as to how God could let evil things happen is partly explained in the Jewish view of human nature. This says that humans are born with free will and the consequence of this is that we have the capacity for evil as well as the capacity for good. Yetzer haTov (good inclination) and yetzer haRa (evil inclination) are equally balanced and people have the choice to follow whichever inclination they choose. However, according to the Kabbalah (the Jewish mystical teachings), creation caused a disunity in the world and divine sparks were scattered throughout the universe. Humanity's task is to repair the world. This is known as tikkun olam (repairing the universe). All humans should therefore regard their good deeds as pushing the world's balance towards good, and their bad deeds as pushing the world towards evil.

The Jewish response to God, despite human suffering, is one of gratitude. This is most obviously expressed on a day-to-day basis in the form of blessings. These take many forms for many purposes, but on a regular basis there are blessings known as birkhot hanehenin (blessings of the senses). These are said before and after eating food, on seeing beautiful things in nature, seeing a rainbow, meeting a learned person and on many other occasions. There is a tradition that says a person should say a hundred blessings a day. Most Jews believe this is not difficult, as there are so many ways to give thanks for God's goodness.

Why you need to know these facts

Judaism is often referred to as a religion of 'ethical monotheism'. This means that belief in God and ethical values go together – you can't have one without the other. For Jews, ethical and moral values are the necessary responses to God. Teaching about God in Judaism enables children to explore their own ideas of God and compare them to the Jewish understanding.

Vocabulary

Covenant – an agreement made between God and humanity when, in return for God's blessing, humanity agrees to keep God's laws.

Noahide Code – seven commandments given to Noah for the whole of humanity; they are: worship only one God, don't blaspheme God, don't commit adultery, don't steal, don't commit murder, practise justice, be kind to animals.

Torah – 'instruction' or 'teaching'; the first five books of the Tenakh.

Sensitive issues

● For many Jewish writers and thinkers the Holocaust, in which six million Jews were murdered, has meant an enormous challenge in thinking about God. There is a minority that believes, after the Holocaust, that God is dead. It is just not possible to conceive of a God who could have allowed this to happen. Others, however, have seen the Holocaust as an extreme example of human evil and that if human beings have free will, as we have discussed, then humanity has freedom to choose evil as well as good.

● Jews seldom write the word God. Often they might write G-d. This is out of respect for the perfection and 'otherness' of God. Using someone's name is an indication of knowing them; humans cannot fully know God.

- After God's covenants with the Jews, they became known as the chosen people. It is very important to point out that this notion of 'chosenness' does not indicate superiority.

Common misconceptions

Despite this ancient history of the Jews, it is inappropriate to see Judaism as merely a religion of the Old Testament. Such a view denies over 2000 years of development. Also it is incorrect to see Judaism as merely a forerunner of Christianity. Judaism is a living religion in its own right with its own view of God, humanity and the relationship between them and the world at large.

Teaching ideas

- Explore with the children what God might be like. Get them to do a short piece of writing describing what God means to them. Look at some descriptions of God in the Psalms, for example Psalms 27, 29, 33, 34 or 47. You could perhaps get the children to paint pictures based on some of these descriptions.
- Ask the children to copy out and illustrate some Jewish blessings.
- Get the children to write their own blessings relevant to their daily lives. Form a class book of blessings and, maybe, read one out together each day.

Torah

Subject facts

What is the Torah?
The Torah (meaning 'instruction' or 'teaching') is, for Jews, the most concrete evidence that God communicates with humanity. It contains an account of God's involvement in history but, most importantly, it also includes instructions as to how God wants people to live.

Basically, the Torah is the five biblical books of Moses: Genesis, Exodus, Leviticus, Numbers and Deuteronomy. These books contain early Jewish history, and commandments and teachings covering every aspect of human existence and relationships with God, other people and the Earth. However, 'the Torah' can also refer to teachings about these books: running parallel with the written Torah is the oral Torah – teachings and interpretations of the written word. They were originally passed on by word of mouth but have been written down for about 2000 years.

Different Jewish groups differ in their views of both the written and the oral Torah. Orthodox Jews view the written Torah as the revealed word of God and the oral Torah as authoritative interpretations, beginning with Moses and handed down to his successors. Reform Jews regard both written and oral Torah as products of their historical and cultural context, although they do regard the written Torah as divinely inspired.

For home study, the Torah is printed in book form, but the Torah is written on scrolls for use in the synagogue. These scrolls are usually called the **Sefer Torah**, because they are hand-written by a sefer (scribe). Sefardi and Ashkenazi scrolls are different. The Sefardi scrolls are kept in a heavy metal or wooden case. The wooden rollers around which the scroll is wound are called the 'trees of life'. Ashkenazi scrolls have an embroidered cloth covering them. They also have silver bells on top of them and an ornament called a breastplate is fitted over the covering.

The Tenakh includes not only the Torah but also Nevi'im (prophetical writings) and Ketuvim (writings such as Psalms, Proverbs and Song of Songs). The word Tenakh derives from an acronym based on the initial letters of the three elements: Torah, Nevi'im and Ketuvim.

Practices connected with the Torah

There are a variety of practices connected with the Torah that illustrate its importance in Jewish life. These are:

- Jews are encouraged to study the Torah regularly. Children study the Torah from about five years of age at the heder (a school normally attached to a synagogue).
- Synagogue services include regular reading from the Torah as a central part of the service.

- The Torah scroll is placed in a large cupboard called the Ark. The scrolls (for there is usually more than one Torah in the synagogue) are ornately 'dressed' with decorated mantles and silver ornaments.
- Before and after the Torah reading, the scrolls are paraded around the synagogue. As the Torah is paraded past them, Jews kiss the fringe of their **tallit** (prayer shawl) and touch the scroll with the fringe.
- Worshippers always stand for the procession and certain readings. Sefardi Jews elevate the scroll before reading and Ashkenazi Jews after the reading.
- Each year at the conclusion of the festival of Sukkot (see page 169) Jews celebrate **Simhat Torah** (rejoicing in the Torah). The scrolls are processed around the synagogue, during the evening service with exuberant dancing and singing.

Mitzvot

The Torah communicates to humanity how God wants people to live. This means living a life of holiness according to God's mitzvot (commandments). Traditionally, there are said to be 613 mitzvot and these can be classified in several ways. Firstly, some are stated in a positive way – 'feed the hungry' – and some in a negative way – 'don't steal'. Mitzvot can also be divided into those that govern relationships between people – 'comfort those in mourning', 'visit the sick' – and those that govern relationships between people and God – 'put a **mezuzah** on the door', 'wear the **tefillin** on weekdays', 'observe the Shabbat'. In one interpretation of mitzvot the 613 are divided up into 365 negative (to correspond to the days of the year) and 248 positive (to correspond to the parts of the human body). In other words, the commandments govern every part of human existence.

Why you need to know these facts

As the Torah is the basis of Jewish belief and practice, a knowledge of its contents, meaning within the tradition and use in worship is vital to understanding the religion. The common theme of the human need for guidance and rules is an important human experience dimension to the study of the Torah.

Vocabulary

Mezuzah – a small box nailed to the right-hand doorposts in a Jewish home, containing verses from Deuteronomy 6: 4–11 and 11: 13–21.

Sefer Torah – the Torah scrolls, handwritten by a scribe called a sefer.

Simhat Torah – the last day of the festival of Sukkot, which marks the end of the yearly readings from the Torah. It is a day of rejoicing and thanking God for the Torah.

Tallit – a prayer shawl worn by Orthodox Jewish men.

Tefillin – two small boxes, worn by Orthodox men, containing words from the Torah. One is bound to the forehead and the other to the left arm adjacent to the heart.

Sensitive issues

Torah scrolls are treated with enormous respect. Although small artefacts of Sefer Torah are available for use in school, be careful to treat these artefacts carefully, perhaps using a yad (pointer) when reading them. Although they are not sacred objects like the real scrolls, it is a good teaching point to treat the artefact with respect.

Common misconceptions

Teachers are sometimes a little confused about what the Torah is. We have discussed narrow and broader definitions of the term. In the broadest sense, the Torah is the whole of traditional Jewish teaching. In the narrow sense, the Torah is the scrolls in the synagogue and the first section of the Hebrew Bible. They are one and the same thing.

Teaching ideas

- The rollers of the Torah scrolls are topped with rimmonim (silver pomegranate-shaped ornaments). It is said that a pomegranate has 613 seeds, the number of mitzvot in the Torah.
- When Sefer Torah scrolls become old, they are buried rather than destroyed. This emphasises the sacred nature of the Torah.
- Arrange a class visit to a synagogue where the children can be shown the Sefer Torah scrolls.
- Show the children artefacts of the Torah.
- The children could make models of the scrolls and/or copy out some Hebrew writing from the Torah. They could learn the Hebrew alphabet.
- Read stories from the Torah that inform the children about the nature of God and God's relationship to humanity and the Jewish people, for example Creation, Abraham and Moses.
- Look at the Ten Commandments; discuss their meaning and why people need rules and guidance. Get the children to write their own set of commandments for today. Alternatively, get the children to write a list of positive and negative mitzvot for the class.

Jewish values

Subject facts

Keeping the mitzvot forms part of the **Halakhah** (law) and is very important spiritually for the Jewish tradition. For Jews, spirituality is the process of bringing **kedusha** (the holiness of God) into everyday life. In studying the Torah and keeping the commandments, a particular Jewish lifestyle emerges. In this lifestyle certain values are seen as important. These values reflect the strong Jewish belief that it is humanity's task to build a better world: to repair the universe.

Love

The first value is that of love. This is expressed in the Torah as the 'golden rule', namely:

You shall love your fellow as yourself.

Leviticus 19: 18

It is also beautifully expressed in an old **Hasidic** saying:

To love God truly, one must first love humanity. And if anyone claims to love God and does not love people, you may be sure it is a lie.

God is often called haRahaman (the compassionate one). In the Torah and in prayers God's love for creation and humanity is constantly mentioned. For example, the Shema (see page 141) emphasises that, in return for God's love, people should love God.

In Jewish thought, loving actions are commanded. This is because it is believed that, even if a feeling of love does not exist, the practice of acting in a loving way will enable love to grow. In Hebrew the name for loving actions is *gemilut hasadim*. This involves all kinds of things like providing 'meals on wheels', visiting the sick, reading for blind people and running holiday camps for disadvantaged children.

Justice

Justice is a very important value in Jewish life. Much of the Halakhah (the civil and religious laws of Judaism) is concerned with bringing justice into the world. 'Justice' in Jewish thought has a broad meaning, but the key element is the just distribution of resources. The Jewish word for charity, tzedakah, refers to justice in this sense. Therefore to give to charity is to act justly. Consequently, those who have more than they need are expected to give to those who have less than they need. This is not an act of kindness but one of justice. The commandment to practise justice is part of the Noahide Code.

Holiness

It is recorded in Torah that God said to Moses:

Say to all the congregation of the people of Israel, You shall be holy; for I the Lord your God am holy.

Leviticus 19: 1

Holiness, kedusha, is very important for Jews. The word means 'separate' or 'distinct' and refers to the 'otherness' of God. Humans cannot fully know the holiness of God but can adopt certain attitudes and behaviour that can bring some of the holiness of God into the world. For example, regular prayer and the saying of blessings, or actions performed lovingly.

There are also many symbolic reminders of holiness for Jews: the tallit and tefillin worn during prayer; the mezuzah on the door to remind people of the presence of God; the kasher food; symbolic lights, such as the **Ner Tamid** (the eternal light found in the synagogue).

Why you need to know these facts

To understand Judaism it is not enough simply to learn about what Jews believe. The Halakhah on its own remains unfulfilled if not put into practice. This putting into practice, and the values that are associated with this, is what is known as the spirituality of the Halakhah. Children need to learn about how Jews practise love, justice and holiness. This will also help them to understand the nature of God and humanity according to Jewish belief.

Vocabulary

Halakhah – 'the way'; the legal teachings of traditional Judaism.
Hasidic – 'pious one'; a sect of Judaism, founded in the 18th century in Eastern Europe. The tradition emphasises joyous worship and a mystical relationship with God. Hasidic Judaism tends to emphasise mystical experience above study of the Torah and hence is rejected by some Orthodox groups.
Kashrut – the Jewish dietary laws derived from Leviticus and Deuteronomy.
Kedusha – holiness, particularly bringing something of the holiness of God into the world.
Kosher – 'proper'; describes food fit to eat according to Jewish dietary laws.
Ner Tamid – the eternal light found in the synagogue.

Sensitive issues

Prejudical views have sometimes stereotyped Jews as being particularly concerned about earning money and that all Jewish people are rich. It is important not to stereotype Jewish people in this way. It is therefore significant that the American-Jewish poet Danny Siegel has done a lot of work trying to find different ways of giving tzedakah (see page 149) that don't involve money. An example would be personal acts of kindness.

Common misconceptions

Sometimes people are not quite clear about the meaning of *tzedakah*. Because it is often translated as 'charity', it is sometimes thought that tzedakah is given simply because someone is needy. But the best way to give tzedakah is to put someone in a position where they won't need it any more, by giving him or her a job, for example. If this can't be done, it is important that the receiver isn't embarrassed. It really is not a matter of charity but of justice; making sure everyone has enough.

Teaching ideas

● Organise a collection for a local 'cause'.
● Explore with the children ideas about loving actions, with examples from their own lives. Get them to write their own examples. Compile a class book of loving actions with written work and illustrations.
● Learn about aspects of Jewish life that bring holiness into the world. This could be prayer, study of the Torah, the laws of **kashrut** or other aspects of Jewish home life.
● Hold a discussion on how people can make the world a better place.

Family life

Subject facts

The family is at the centre of Jewish life and Jews see the family as essential to the maintenance and transmission of Jewish values and heritage. The home is often referred to as Mikdash Me'at (little sanctuary) and is the centre of religious life. There are several elements that identify a Jewish home and it is worth emphasising two here.

Mezuzah

It is written in Deuteronomy 6:9, 'and you shall write [these words] on the doorpost of your house and gates'. The words are the words of the Shema (see page 141) and the mezuzah (literally, doorpost) fulfils this commandment. The mezuzah is a small box containing the Shema (written on a small piece of parchment) that is nailed to the right-hand doorpost of each door in the house. Many Jews will reach up to touch the mezuzah when they enter the house or a room in the house. This is to remind them that their lives should be lived in accordance with the words contained inside the mezuzah. Written on the back of the parchment is the word Shaddai, meaning almighty. It also stands for the initial letters of Shomer Daltot Israel (the Guardian of the Doors of Israel). In this sense, the mezuzah represents the protection of the household by God.

Kashrut

For Orthodox families it is extremely important to keep the laws of kashrut (fitness) – the laws that govern the food Jews can eat. The laws of kashrut are given in the Torah in Leviticus 11. The first group of rules is about what foods are considered to be kasher (fit, proper). These are: all plants, fruits and vegetables, mammals with split hooves and which chew the cud, fish with both scales and fins, all domestic birds, the milk of any kasher mammal and the eggs of any kasher bird. The second set of rules governs the killing of animals for food.

Jews kill animals for food by a method they believe to be most humane – stunning an animal is not allowed, rather the animal's throat should receive a single cut of a very sharp knife. This ritual slaughter is called shehitah and the person who carries out the task a shohet. Jews believe that the 'spirit of life' is contained in the blood of all creatures and so all blood is drained from the meat before it is eaten.

The laws of kashrut also include restrictions about the way in which meat and milk are used. First, meat and milk must not be cooked together:

> You shall not boil a kid in the milk of its mother.
>
> Exodus 23: 19

Second, meat and milk products must not be eaten together (no cheeseburgers!). Third, meat and milk must not be used together. In many Orthodox kitchens there are separate sets of cooking utensils, cutlery and cloths to ensure the rules are kept.

Reform or Liberal families keep these laws at different levels. Some secular Jews tend not to keep them at all.

Shabbat (Sabbath)

For Jews, the most important festival is celebrated at home every week – Shabbat (the Sabbath). As we have seen, it is vitally important for Jews to bring the holiness of God (kedusha) into everyday life. One way this is done is by making time holy or sacred. The commandment to keep Shabbat occurs twice in the Torah – in Exodus and Deuteronomy. In Exodus, Shabbat is connected with creation and the seventh day, when God created a day of rest and repose. The second reference is connected with the freedom from slavery in Egypt. Therefore Shabbat commemorates both the creation of the universe by God and God's historical relationship with the Jewish people.

Shabbat begins at sunset on Friday evening and finishes at sunset on Saturday. The meal served on Friday is preceded by three days of preparation, spiritual as well as physical. On Friday the house is cleaned, any remaining shopping is done, the food is prepared for the three meals eaten during Shabbat and then family members wash and change into clean clothes. Just before the sun sets, the mother and children light the Shabbat candles. They are lit just before sunset because the Torah forbids the lighting of fire on the Sabbath. Once lit, the mother draws the light from the candles up towards her face, in a symbolic gesture made three to seven times. She covers her eyes with her hands and says the blessing:

> Blessed are You, Lord our God, King of the universe, who has sanctified us with His commandments and commanded us to light the Shabbat candles.

The light should be put to some good use like reading or eating the meal, otherwise it is deemed to be wasted and the blessing invalid.

Other members of the family will attend the synagogue for a short evening service on the Friday evening. When they return, the greetings 'Gut Shabbos' or 'Shabbat Shalom' are exchanged, a passage from the book of Proverbs that praises the model wife is read, and the children receive a blessing. **Kiddush**, a special prayer and blessing, is then recited over a full goblet of wine to symbolise the joy of Shabbat. After Kiddush the family wash their hands and remove the cover from the two **challah** loaves. It is said that the cover symbolises the dew on the ground when God provided the Jews with manna in the desert. There are two loaves to symbolise the double portion of manna found on Fridays, so they would not have to gather it on Shabbat. Traditionally, the bread is broken, sprinkled with salt and passed around the table. The Friday night meal then follows – usually the best meal of the week and often the one when the whole family can get together – and songs are sung. Sometimes guests are invited to share in this joyous occasion.

On Saturday morning many Jews will attend the Shabbat service in the synagogue. On returning home there is another meal preceded by Kiddush and again traditional songs are sung. The afternoon may be spent in such activities as study, conversation or walking with the family. Shabbat concludes, just after nightfall, with the beautiful **Havdalah** ceremony: a plaited candle is lit, blessings are said over wine and spices and then the candle is put out with a drop of wine. In this way it is hoped that the sweet smell of Shabbat will influence the early days of the week before preparation for the next Shabbat starts.

Why you need to know these facts

Shabbat is a wonderful resource for children to 'learn from' religion. It is the most important day of the week, so much so that the working week revolves around it and not the other way round. Shabbat challenges us to think about what is important in life. Rabbi Hugo Grynn said, 'Shabbat teaches us that whilst we may own our possessions, our possessions don't own us.' In other words, the material world has its place but it must not dominate a person's life; far more important is time for each other and time for God. Such thinking is a great challenge to modern life.

Vocabulary

Challah – loaves used on Shabbat and festivals.
Havdalah – separation; a ceremony that marks the end of Shabbat and festivals. It is made over wine, spices and the light of a plaited candle.
Kiddush – sanctification; a prayer that proclaims the holiness of Shabbat and festivals. It is recited before meals over a cup of wine.

Sensitive issues

Much of what is written in this section refers to the practice of Orthodox Judaism. It is important to remember that Jewish practice differs over things such as keeping the laws of kashrut. Reform and Progressive Jews tend to observe the laws at different levels. Non-religious Jews may not observe some laws at all.

Common misconceptions

Unlike the other religions, being a Jew is a cultural identity that can include being religious, but not necessarily so. The only other religion anything like that is Hinduism, where again culture and religion are very closely intertwined. Not all Jews, therefore, are religious. Being Jewish is for some as much about cultural identity as it is a matter of religion. Even though they may not be religious, some Jews will follow Jewish traditions in their family life.

Teaching ideas

- Talk about what makes home special for the children.
- Discuss and write about special times connected with the home.
- Learn about the mezuzah and why it is special for Jews. Children could make their own.
- Show the children some of the special objects used during Shabbat. Ask the children to investigate how the objects are used.
- Bring in examples of kosher and non-kosher foods, and show the children a picture of a Jewish kitchen. Talk about why some foods are permitted and others not. Children could make a poster showing kosher foods.

Life rituals

Subject facts

Like all religions, Judaism has a number of rituals and celebrations marking significant stages in a person's life and the role that God plays in them.

Brit Milah

Brit Milah (covenant of circumcision) is a sign of the covenant made between God and Abraham, the first Patriarch or father of Judaism. Abraham is believed to be the first man to teach faith in one God and is therefore seen as the father of the Jewish people. Brit Milah is a duty prescribed in Genesis 17: 10–11.

Brit Milah must take place on the eighth day after the boy's birth, even if the day is Shabbat or a festival day. (In a few cases there might be medical reasons for delaying the circumcision but, even if there is a delay, the ceremony can take place on Shabbat or a holy day.) It can take place anywhere; at home, in the hospital or, sometimes, in the synagogue. If possible, the ceremony should take place in the presence of a **minyan** (a quorum of ten adult males required for community prayer).

The ceremony is usually performed by a mohel – a person trained in the Halakhah (law) and medical hygiene – and it is the father's responsibility to see that the circumcision is carried out. In some families, the father stays awake the night before the circumcision to study the Torah. Traditionally, the mother is not in the room for the circumcision, although amongst some Progressive Jews the mother is there and shares in some of the ritual.

On the morning of the circumcision candles are lit in the room and, after morning prayers, friends and relations bring the child into the room. He is placed on a pillow on the 'chair of Elijah' – the prophet Elijah is said to attend every circumcision and a special chair is set aside for him. The baby is held by the sandek (godfather), who is the only person seated while the mohel performs the operation. At the start of the ceremony, the mohel urges Elijah to 'stand at my right and sustain me'. After the circumcision has been performed, the baby's Hebrew names are announced. A simple meal and a gathering usually follow the ceremony, at which members of all generations of the family get together.

Girl's naming ceremony

There is no circumcision for girls. In Orthodox families, on the Shabbat after the birth of a daughter, the father is called up to read the Torah in the synagogue. Prayers are recited for mother and baby and the name of the girl is announced. In Progressive circles, in addition to the Brit, both boys and girls are brought to the synagogue for a special blessing on a Shabbat shortly after birth. The parents bring the baby forward to the **Aron Hakodesh** (the 'Holy Ark' where the Torah scrolls are kept). Prayers are said for the welfare of mother and child and the blessing from Numbers 6: 24–26 is recited over the baby.

Every baby is given a Hebrew name in addition to any name known for general purposes. This name consists of the given name (at the Brit for the boy or naming ceremony for the girl) plus the name of the father, in some cases also the mother. An example would be Sarah bat Yirmiyahu, which means Sarah daughter of Jeremy. Ashkenazi Jews will name a child after a dead relative and generally avoid using the name of a living relative. Sefardi tend to do the opposite and use the name of an honoured living relative.

Bar/Bat Mitzvah

Bar Mitzvah (son of the commandment) and Bat Mitzvah (daughter of the commandment) is a time for boys and girls to take on adult responsibilities in terms of their religious life. Originally this ceremony took place when the child was counted as an adult in terms of sexual maturity – nowadays, this has become standardized to 13 for boys and 12 for girls. The main significance of Bar or Bat Mitzvah is that the young person now becomes fully responsible for fulfilling the mitzvot of the Torah and the ceremony is connected with the Torah.

For a boy, the ceremony is held as soon as possible after his thirteenth birthday. At a synagogue service at which the Torah is read (which means on a Monday, Thursday, Shabbat, festival or new-moon day) a boy is called up to read the Torah, usually the last section which includes the **Haftarah** (the portion from the prophets). The boy may also lead some parts of the morning service. Afterwards, a special meal is held and the boy may give a D'var Torah – a commentary on some words of the Torah.

For a girl, the ceremony does not include reading from the Torah in the synagogue. This reflects the Orthodox view that the roles of men and women are equal but different. It is not necessary for a woman to attend the synagogue service as it is for men. There are some exceptions to this in America, where some Jewish groups hold women-only synagogue services. In that case a Bat Mitzvah may well resemble the ceremony for boys. Nevertheless, in the UK an Orthodox girl is likely to prepare a D'var Torah, which is given at a later part of the service or during Kiddush after the end of the service. Progressive Jews tend not to make a distinction between how a Bar or Bat Mitzvah is celebrated.

Marriage

For Jews, marriage is seen as an ideal and a positive duty. Marriage is regarded as holy, as can be seen from the Torah. Jewish weddings can take place out in the open, at home or in a synagogue. On the Shabbat before the wedding, the bridegroom may be called upon to read from the Torah. Afterwards those present may call out 'mazal tov' (good luck). In some synagogues raisins or sweets are thrown to symbolise good wishes. Some couples will fast on the day of the wedding until after the ceremony. On the wedding day the bride and her attendants wait in a special room in the synagogue and are visited there by the groom. He recites a blessing to his bride to be:

O sister, be the mother of thousands and ten thousands.

He then covers her face with a veil, which remains until after the ceremony. The ceremony itself takes place under a huppah – a canopy made of wood, with embroidered cloth stretched over it and usually decorated with flowers. There are a variety of meanings associated with the huppah: it is said to symbolise the couple's new home; it is open to the sky to remind the couple that God promised Abraham his descendants would be as numerous as the stars in the sky; and it is a reminder of the tent that was set aside in ancient times for new brides and grooms. In some cases a couple will prefer to have a tallit (prayer shawl) held over them.

To begin the ceremony the groom's father and future father-in-law lead the groom to the huppah. The bride's mother and mother-in-law do the same for the bride. At least two other adults, witnesses to the wedding, join this party under the huppah. The **rabbi** then recites two blessings and a cup of wine is shared between the bride and groom. The groom places a gold ring on the index finger of the bride's right hand, saying:

Behold you are betrothed to me with this ring, according to the law of Moses and of Israel. By accepting the ring the bride has consented to the marriage.

Next, the **ketubah** is read by the couple. This is a legal document that reminds the couple of their responsibilities towards each other; it is usually highly decorated. Two witnesses sign the ketubah and the bride keeps it as proof of her marriage. Seven blessings are chanted over a full cup of wine, which is then shared by the bride and the groom. For this there must be a minyan. One blessing reads:

Bring great rejoicing on these loving companions as you brought rejoicing on your first creation in the Garden of Eden. Blessed are you, O Lord, who brings rejoicing to bridegroom and bride.

Finally, a wineglass wrapped in a cloth is broken under the groom's foot. Some say this symbolises the destruction of the temple by the Romans. Some look at this ritual as reminding the couple that married life can have its 'downs' as well as its good side. Whatever the case, the ritual emphasises the fragility and precious nature of human life. Those couples who have fasted now go to a room to break the fast and a celebratory meal follows.

Death

Jews believe that there is life after death, but that the important thing is to serve God in this life because it is the kind of person you are in this life that determines what happens to you when you die. Jews do not tend to bother with theories about life after death, because only God can know this. The important thing is to concentrate on fulfilling the mitzvot.

When it is obvious that a person is dying, prayers are said and the dying person will try to recite the Shema. When a person has died, news of the death is greeted with a blessing:

> Blessed are you, Lord our God, King of the universe,
> the true judge.

Close relatives often tear a garment, an action called keriah. Nowadays, this is a public indication of mourning.

After death, the body is ritually washed by members of the local community called the hevra kadisha (holy society). Although Jews believe the soul leaves the body at death, the body is respected and members of the hevra kadisha stay with the body from the moment of death until the burial. The body is dressed in simple white garments and placed in a coffin. Men are normally buried with their tallit (prayer shawl) wrapped around the shroud and one of the fringes cut off to signify the final nature of the event.

Most Jewish communities have their own cemetery or separate section in the public cemetery. There is usually a small prayer house where part of the funeral service is held; the rest of the service will take place by the side of the grave. After the coffin has been lowered into the grave, every person helps put in some earth. This reminds the mourners of the reality of death. The mourners chant, 'may he/she come to his/her place in peace'. It is customary to remain at the graveside until the coffin is covered or the grave is filled. Before leaving, mourners wash their hands in a special basin. Orthodox Jews do not practise cremation because they believe in a physical resurrection, when the soul will be restored to the body. Some Reform and Liberal Jews do practise cremation. Many Jews may well donate healthy organs for transplants. This reflects the Jewish belief that it is important to help save the lives of others.

Mourning

Once the funeral has taken place, mourning begins. Friends of the mourners prepare a meal and special foods are eaten. For example, eggs are eaten as a symbol of life and fertility but also, because they are round, as a symbol of the cycle of life, which includes death.

During the first week after the funeral, the family stays at home and friends visit to offer comfort, share grief or just sit quietly. Visitors may bring food or do the shopping. Enough people to form a minyan will visit, in order that the community memorial prayer, called the kaddish, can be said. The kaddish is about life and the holiness of God.

After the week of mourning is over, the family goes back to normal life but family members do not go to parties or other celebrations for three weeks. Every day they will say the kaddish in their prayers. If the mourning is for a father or mother then it lasts for another ten months; this is to signify the importance of the child-parent relationship. Kaddish is said every year on the anniversary of the death.

Why you need to know these facts

● The rituals of death and mourning are important because they help Jewish people not only to show respect for the dead but to 'work through' their feelings and to place their trust in God.
● Jewish people think of their religion as a 'religion of life'. The Torah, for example, is often called the 'tree of life' because Jews believe that the Torah contains all the instructions they need to live the good life that God intends for human beings. Jews believe that what human beings do is of enormous value to God and that life itself is God's precious gift to humanity. The life rituals that

Judaism

Jews celebrate and mark as a family and community are a deep expression of these truths and values. The underlying belief that the cycle of life is a natural part of God's will is a key area for making connections between Jewish belief and practice and our shared human experience.

Vocabulary

Aron Hakodesh – Holy Ark; the cupboard in the eastern wall of a synagogue in which the Torah scrolls are kept.
Haftarah – completion; the portion from the writings of the prophets which is read in the synagogue on Shabbat, after the reading of the Torah.
Ketubah – the wedding document detailing the rights of the wife.
Minyan – quorum of ten adult males required for community prayer.
Rabbi – teacher; usually applied to any graduate from a seminary. Originally it applied to any wise teacher.

Amazing facts

The Jewish rabbis who lived 2000 years ago made a list which set out parental responsibilities to children. These include the responsibilities of circumcising a boy child, teaching children the Torah, teaching them a trade, helping them to find someone to marry, and some rabbis included teaching them to swim!

Common misconceptions

It is not uncommon for a non-Jew to look for reasons for commandments, for example keeping the laws of kashrut or circumcising a child. Some people might say that rules such as these are for health reasons, for example. An Orthodox Jew would dispute this. They believe that a person should obey the mitzvot simply because God has said so. They believe it is not humankind's place to question the will of God.

Teaching ideas

● Explore the idea of promises. Get the children to think of promises that are important to keep. Make a class book of promises.

● Look at certificates that contain promises, such as for Brownies, Guides and Cubs, and get the children to design their own Jewish marriage certificate.

● Read the story of the covenant with Abraham (Genesis 15–16).

● Discuss with the children things they do out of duty, for example visiting their grandparents. Explore the link with circumcision and the idea that people often have to obey a sense of duty.

● Consider at what ages the children take on special responsibilities and relate this to learning about the Bar or Bat Mitzvah.

● Re-enact a Jewish wedding.

● Get the children to draw and illustrate a special ketubah that outlines promises they think a couple should make.

The synagogue

Subject facts

We have mentioned ways in which Jews make time holy. Another important aspect of kedusha (bringing the holiness of God into the world) is through making places holy or sacred. Jews believe that by doing holy things they can make places holy.

The word synagogue means 'meeting place'. The synagogue is also known by three other names, describing the main purposes of the building. These are Bet Tifillah (the house of prayer), Bet Knesset (the house of meeting) and Bet Midrash (the house of study). Orthodox and Reform synagogues differ in their arrangements in the prayer hall.

In an Orthodox synagogue, men and women will sit separately, with the women often seated in a gallery upstairs. Men will wear the tallit (prayer shawl) and, in both Orthodox and Reform synagogues, the kippah (headcovering). In Reform synagogues (see Figure 5) people all sit together and the **bimah** (the desk from where the Torah is read) is at the front, rather than in the middle, as is the practice for Orthodox Jews.

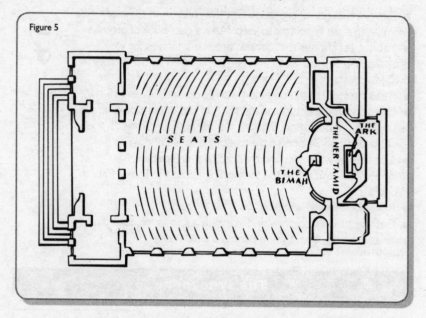

Figure 5

Most synagogues have a number of personnel. The rabbi (teacher) acts as a teacher of the Torah and is expected to be knowledgeable enough to advise members on the Halakhah (law). He also offers spiritual advice but is not a priest in the sense of having a sacramental role. Orthodox rabbis are always men but Progressive Jews have both men and women rabbis. In Orthodox synagogues there may also be a **hazzan** or cantor, who has the job of leading the prayers throughout most of the service.

Sabbath service – the house of prayer

The most important service of the week is the Shabbat service. In Orthodox synagogues this can take up to two hours and includes prayers and readings from the appropriate portion of the Torah. After recitation of the Morning Prayer, the Aron Hakodesh (Ark of the Covenant) is opened and the Torah scroll is taken out and processed around the synagogue to the bimah. The congregation stands as the scrolls are carried. The portion for the week is then chanted and seven members of the congregation are called up to recite the blessings before and after each section of the reading. This is regarded as an honour and is called Aliyah (going up). After the service, Kiddush is said in a hall in the synagogue. Some verses from the Torah, which tell about the keeping of Shabbat, are sung. Then a blessing is said over the wine, often by the rabbi, and everyone has a drink of wine and eats cakes and biscuits. Lively conversation takes place and any visitors are welcomed. Sometimes a family who may be celebrating a special event, such as a birth in the family, will provide the wine and biscuits. Kiddush reflects the idea of the synagogue being Bet Knesset, the house of meeting.

The house of meeting
Many Jews will also meet at the synagogue at other times in the week; this may involve social or educational groups. People may also come to visit the rabbi for personal advice.

The house of study
Most synagogues will provide educational programmes. Because study of the Torah is an essential way of bringing God's holiness into the world, Jewish communities set up heder (religious schools), which are usually attached to the synagogue. Children normally start going to heder at the age of five and continue up to the age of Bar or Bat Mitzvah. They go to the heder on Sunday mornings and weekday evenings. Some synagogues also hold adult classes on Sunday mornings.

Why you need to know these facts

Living as a community is very important for Jewish people. Judaism as a religion tends not to make a sharp distinction between sacred and secular activities. Therefore activities that take place in a synagogue, such as community action and social care, are as important as the study of the Torah. When teaching about this in RE it is important to explore the role of community in people's lives and how meeting together regularly and taking part in shared activities can enrich life and give it meaning.

Judaism

Vocabulary

Bimah – desk from where the Torah is read.
Hazzan – cantor; a person who leads prayer using traditional tunes.

Sensitive issues

If you want to visit a synagogue with the class, try to avoid Fridays as people will be getting ready for Shabbat. Also try to avoid festival times. Check with the Shap calendar: **www.shapworkingparty.org.uk**.
Note: all men need to cover their heads in the synagogue.

Amazing facts

● A small Jewish community was established in Britain after the Norman Conquest in 1066 but was expelled in 1290. Jewish people were readmitted in the 17th century. The oldest synagogue in use in Britain today is the Bevis Marks Synagogue in London, built in 1701.
● Despite the importance of the synagogue to the Jewish community, it is not regarded as a holy place or consecrated building. Its importance lies in its three main functions and it is what goes on in the building and amongst people connected with the building that is holy.

Teaching ideas

● Discuss with the children any groups to which they belong and any meetings that are held. List the reasons why they think it is important to meet together.
● If possible, arrange for a Jewish guide to show you round the synagogue when you visit.

● Discuss with the children the meanings of objects that can be found inside a synagogue, such as Aron Hakodesh, Ner Tamid and bimah. As a class, learn about activities that take place in the synagogue other than prayer and study.

● Arrange the classroom to look like a synagogue and get some of the boys to read passages from the Torah. Hold a Kiddush at the end.

Festivals

Subject facts

For Jews, the notion of sacred time is very important. It is very important for Jews to set aside time throughout the year in order to remember God in every part of life. By setting aside 'holy time', by making places and people holy, Jews remember that they should strive to be kehilla kedosha (a holy community). The many Jewish festivals celebrate different aspects of Jewish life and history, and the Jewish relationship with God. The pilgrim festivals, Pesach, Shavu'ot and Sukkot, and the festivals of the New Year, Rosh Hashanah and Yom Kippur, are celebrated because God, communicating through the Torah, said that these times should be set apart.

There are other festivals, such as **Purim** and **Hanukkah**, and other fasts and anniversaries that have not been laid down in the Torah but are celebrated to commemorate some important aspect of Jewish life or history. It is the Torah festivals that we shall concentrate on here. The Jewish year starts in the month of Tishri, the Jewish month that occurs in September. The Jews use a lunar calendar.

Festivals of the Torah

There are three festivals of the Torah, often known as pilgrim festivals: Pesach, Shavu'ot and Sukkot. They are called pilgrim festivals because they were times when Jewish people were commanded to go on pilgrimage to Jerusalem. It is written in the Torah that:

> *Three times a year, at Pesach, at Shavu'ot and at Sukkot, all your*
> *males shall appear before the Lord your God in the place that*
> *He will choose.*
>
> Deuteronomy 6: 16

All three festivals have an agricultural as well as historical significance.

Pesach

Pesach is celebrated on the 15th to the 21st of Nisan (the
Hebrew month that coincides with April/May). Agriculturally,
Pesach celebrates the beginning of the wheat harvest and
lambing time. Historically, and much more significantly for the
Jews, Pesach remembers the Jews' Exodus from Egypt (as told
in Exodus 12: 1–27 and Deuteronomy 16: 1–8). The key Jewish
beliefs about Pesach are that it commemorates the fact that God
has set the Jewish people free and has chosen the Jewish nation
to be his people. The festival lasts for eight days outside of Israel,
whereas in Israel it lasts for a week.

At the centre of Pesach is the **Seder** (order) meal, when the
family retells the story of the Exodus; details of the telling of
the story are found in the book called the **Hagaddah** (retelling).
The Seder is full of symbolism, highlighted by the Seder plate on
which symbolic foods are placed: roasted egg and roasted lamb
shank remember the Paschal sacrifices before the destruction of
the temple; bitter herbs recall the bitterness of slavery; a mixture
known as haroset, made from apples and nuts, symbolises the
mortar used to make bricks by the Israelite slaves in Egypt;
matzah (unleavened bread) is eaten as the bread of slavery and
the bread of freedom. Before Pesach begins, all leavened products
are cleared from the house.

Shavu'ot

Shavu'ot is celebrated on the 6th of Sivan (the Hebrew month
which falls in May/June). Agriculturally, it commemorates the
barley harvest. Historically, it is a celebration of the Torah, in
particular the revelation on Mount Sinai when God gave his
teaching to Moses. Therefore in revealing the Torah to Moses,
God has revealed his will to the Jewish people.

At Shavu'ot the synagogue is decorated with greenery and
flowers. On the festival day, the Ten Commandments are read
during worship in the synagogue and the congregation will stand

in reverence. Many people spend the night before the festival awake, reading and discussing the Torah. During this night a special meal is eaten which includes milk and honey. This refers to the promise from God to Moses that the Promised Land (Israel) would be flowing with milk and honey. These foods are symbols of the Torah as well as the Promised Land. Often honey sweets are given to a child when he or she begins to learn the Torah.

Sukkot

Sukkot is celebrated from the 15th to the 21st of Tishri (the Jewish month that falls in September/October). Agriculturally, it is the final harvest festival, when the people built simple huts in the fields to be near their crops. Historically, it commemorates the Jewish people's wandering in the desert after the Exodus from Egypt. Another name for Sukkot is the Feast of Tabernacles; this refers to the tents that the Jewish people lived in because they did not have permanent homes.

Today, Jewish people build temporary shelters called sukkahs at home and at the synagogue during the festival. These are usually built outside or adjoining one of the outside doors of the house. Greenery is draped over the structure and it is important that the stars can be seen through the roof. This is to remind Jews of the finite nature of human life and that the only truly firm foundation lies with God. Some Jews might live in the sukkah during the eight days of the festival or, alternatively, eat their meals in it.

During the morning service in the synagogue, four plants – palm, myrtle, willow and a yellow citrus fruit called etrog – are waved in all directions. This is commanded in Leviticus 23: 40 and it is an act of rejoicing before God. The last day of the festival is Simhat Torah, which celebrates the giving of the Torah by God to the Jewish people.

Festivals of the New Year

The ten-day period from Rosh Hashanah, New Year, to Yom Kippur, the Day of Atonement, is known as the Days of Awe. These ten days mark a period of repentance and spiritual self-examination, a time when God's sovereignty and humanity's moral responsibility are acknowledged.

Rosh Hashanah

Rosh Hashanah is celebrated on the 1st and 2nd of Tishri (the Jewish month that falls in September/October). It is mentioned in the Torah in Leviticus 22: 23–25 and Numbers 29: 1–6 and is the beginning of the season of repentance and a reminder to Jewish people of the importance of repentance. The Hebrew word for repentance is *teshuvah* (returning).

The festival is linked to three stories in the Torah. The first one is the Creation, when Jews remember how God created the world. It is traditional to share pieces of apple dipped in honey at the Kiddush (see page 154). In this way they are looking back to the creation and forward in the hope of a sweet and happy New Year.

At Rosh Hashanah people also remember that everyone should obey God. Therefore the story of Abraham's readiness to sacrifice his son Isaac is a reminder of such faith. At the festival a ram's horn, called a **shofar**, is blown as way of recalling Abraham's faith.

Finally, the festival also reminds Jewish people of the receiving of the Torah by Moses and its importance in their lives. Many believe that when Moses received the Torah on Mount Sinai people could hear the sound of the blowing of the shofar. The blowing of the shofar today is a call to the heart of each person signifying that in not following the laws of the Torah they need to seek repentance.

Yom Kippur

Ten days after Rosh Hashanah, Jews celebrate the solemn Day of Atonement or Yom Kippur. On this day everybody tries to make amends for their sins and seek repentance. Many Jews stay in the synagogue for the whole day, where there will be five different services of prayer and readings from the Torah. The synagogue will be decorated in white, and many people will dress in white. Fasting and giving to charity are also part of this day for many people. Yom Kippur expresses three significant Jewish beliefs about repentance:

● First, Judaism accepts the fact that people make mistakes in their lives and are capable of hurting themselves and others. It is important, therefore, for people to be able to own up to these mistakes (confession).

● Second, people should repent of their mistakes. Yom Kippur allows people to express sorrow for their mistakes in a collective way. At the services on Yom Kippur the congregation recites Al-Het, which is an alphabetical confession of sins undertaken by the whole congregation so that individuals do not feel isolated and the importance of communal responsibility is recognised.

● Finally, people are encouraged to make amends for their sins. The final service of the day ends with prayers that acknowledge the oneness and kingship of God and the joy of accepting God's repentance. The service and the fast end with a single call of the shofar.

Why you need to know these facts

The idea of sacred time as expressed in these festivals is something essential to understanding the relationship between the Jewish people and God. The idea that God is inexorably linked to humanity in time, space and people is a fundamental message of Judaism. These themes lie at the heart of much of what we are concerned about in RE. The sacredness of life, often not recognised as much today as it once was, has been the central theme of a religious view of life since the dawn of time.

Vocabulary

Hagaddah – retelling; the book used in retelling the Exodus story at the Seder meal on the first evening of the Pesach festival.
Hanukkah – holiday celebrating the rededication of the Temple during the time of the Maccabbees in 165BCE; usually occurs in December.
Purim – holiday celebrating events described in the Book of Esther; occurs in February/March.
Shofar – ram's horn trumpet.

Judaism

Amazing facts

Jewish years are counted from the first Shabbat of Creation. Therefore, according to Jewish tradition (and if you count the years as set out in the Bible), Creation happened in 3760BCE. So in the year 2012, Creation happened 5772 years ago.

Common misconceptions

Although the Jewish calendar is a lunar one, it is not a lunar calendar like, for example, the Muslim calendar. It is a complicated system that means the months move around in comparison with the Christian calendar but stay in the same season. This would not be possible in a purely lunar calendar. Twelve lunar months give a year that is 11 days shorter than the ordinary year. If no adjustment were made the festivals would lose their seasonal associations. Therefore there is a system of leap years in which the last month of the year, Adar, is repeated every two or three years, so that over 19 years, the Jewish year averages 365¼ days.

Teaching ideas

- Focus on the festivals of Pesach and Yom Kippur.
- Read the story of Exodus.
- Discuss with the children which things in the story of Exodus are happy and which are sad.
- Look at artefacts associated with Pesach, especially the Seder plate. Re-enact a short Seder in the classroom.
- Get the children to make their own Seder plates, illustrating them with symbols.
- Collect examples of how people can make mistakes or do wrong things (from newspapers, magazines and so on).
- Collect examples from the children of things they do wrong and for which they feel sorry.

● Use a moment of silence to get the children to think about things in the world for which humans should say sorry. Develop a vocabulary list of bad human characteristics and good characteristics.

● Get the children to write prayers or poems apologising to God for the bad things that humans do.

Resources

Artefacts suppliers
Articles of Faith (see page 33 for details).
Jewish Education Bureau, 8 Westcombe Avenue, Leeds LS8 2BS, 0870 800 8532.
Religion in Evidence (see page 33 for details).

TV programmes (available on DVD)
Channel 4 *Animated World Faiths* series for ages 7–11.

Useful books
Religion in Focus: Judaism by Geoff Teece (Franklin Watts, 2008).
Create and Display: Festivals by Claire Tinker (Scholastic, 2010).

Useful websites
www.holidays.net/highholydays
www.jewfaq.org
www.jewisheducationbureau.co.uk
www.reonline.org.uk
http://retoday.org.uk

Chapter 6

Sikhism

Sikhism is the youngest major religion. Its origins lie in the teachings of Guru Nanak, born in 1469 (see pages 178–81). The word 'Sikh' comes from the Punjabi word *sishya* (disciple or learner). Sikhism is often called the Sikh Dharam (Sikh way of life).

Sikhism is a revealed religion. Sikhs believe it was revealed by God to Guru Nanak and the nine Gurus (see pages 183–6) who succeeded him, and that this revelation is now contained in the holy scriptures – the **Guru Granth Sahib** (see pages 188–9). This revelation is not exclusive – it rejects distinctions of creed, caste, race or sex. Sikhism stresses the oneness of God and equality of all human beings. It is important for Sikhs to act in the service of all people and to tolerate other religions. They believe that to deny their authenticity is to question God's purpose. Guru Amar Das (see page 184) said:

> All are created from the seed of God. There is the same clay in
> the whole world, the potter (God) makes many kinds of pots.
> Page 1128 of The Hymns of Guru Amar Das

There are an estimated 30 million Sikhs in the world, with about 61 per cent of these in the Punjab region of India, the land of the religion's origins. There are Sikh communities around the world, in particular in the United States, Canada, UK, Hong Kong, Singapore, East Africa, Malaysia and India. Estimates of the number of Sikhs in the UK vary between 400,000 and 500,000. There are about 300 **gurdwaras** (Sikh Temples) in the UK.

This chapter introduces the key teachings and practices of Sikhism. There are three main areas: the Gurus, the Sikh community and identity, and Sikh religious practices.

God and the goal of life

Sikhs believe in one God, known by many names. There are many names for God in the Guru Granth Sahib, including names commonly associated with Hindu and Muslim belief. This illustrates the Sikh belief that there is one God for all of humanity. Nevertheless, Sikhs have some particular names for God. The two traditionally used in worship are **Sat Nam** ('the true name', sometimes translated as 'the eternal reality') and **Waheguru** ('wonderful lord').

Sikhs believe that God created the world over a period of time and that creation evolved slowly from lower to higher forms of life. From air came water, from water lower forms of life, which in turn led to the creation of plants, birds and animals. Finally, human beings were created as the highest form of life.

The fundamental Sikh belief about God is found in the **Mool Mantra**, which begins every section of the Guru Granth Sahib. It reads:

Ik	There is but one God
Onkar	He is all pervading
Sat Nam	His Name is everlasting
Karta	He is the Creator
Purukh	He is present throughout His Creation
Nirbhao	He fears nothing
Nirvair	He is without enmity
Akal-Murat	His existence is immortal
Ajuni	He is not born, nor does He die
Swe-Bhang	He is self-illuminated
Gur-Prasad	He is realised through the grace of the Guru

The symbol of Ik Onkar (see Figure 6 on page 176) is commonly found in Sikh gurdwaras and homes.

Figure 6

IK ONKAR

Guru Nanak taught that everything that happens does so according to **hukam** (God's will). Nothing happens outside of the will of God. The goal of life for a Sikh is to progress spiritually from self-centredness to God-centredness. Sikhs use the word **haumai**, which means ego, or I-centredness. Haumai is part of creation because nothing exists outside the will of God. A person who is subjected to haumai is referred to as **manmukh**. It says in the Guru Granth Sahib:

> *Under the compulsion of haumai man comes and goes, is born and dies, gives and takes, earns and loses, speaks truths and lies, smears himself with evil and washes himself of it.*
>
> Guru Granth Sahib

This compulsion is caused by **maya** (delusion). It is the opposite of truth and truthful living. It is ignorance of what is truly real and life enhancing.

Self-centredness leads to the five vices (see page 201). For Sikhs the goal is to become **gurmukh** (God-centred) through a spiritual path of **nam simran** (keeping God constantly in mind) and **sewa** (selfless service on behalf of others) and so become **mukti** (spiritually liberated).

Why you need to know these facts

Sikh beliefs about God cannot be separated from Sikh views about human relationships. A Sikh cannot love God and not love his or her fellow human beings. This belief, of course, results in key Sikh values, such as equality. In the context of RE it is important that children learn about the Sikh view of God and apply that learning to their understanding of human relationships and human values.

Vocabulary

Gurmukh – God-centred or -oriented.
Guru Gobind Singh (1666–1708) – the tenth Sikh Guru and founder of the Khalsa (the community of the pure).
Guru Granth Sahib – Sikh holy scriptures (see pages 188–90).
Haumai – egoism; the major spiritual defect.
Hukam – 'divine order' or the will of God.
Manmukh – self-oriented (as opposed to gurmukh, God-oriented).
Maya – delusion; when the soul identifies itself with physical matter; to be wrong about what is truly real.
Mool Mantra – the basic statement of belief about God at the beginning of the Guru Granth Sahib.
Mukti – spiritually liberated.
Nam simran – keeping God constantly in mind.
Sat Nam – 'the true name;' a popular Sikh name for God.
Sewa – selfless service.
Waheguru – 'wonderful lord'; a popular Sikh name for God.

Amazing facts

Hundreds of years before the Equal Opportunities Act of 1975, the Gurus were revolutionary in their teaching of the equality of men and women. The bestowing of the name 'singh' and 'kaur' on men and women respectively by **Guru Gobind Singh**, indicates the importance of equal status of men and women.

Common misconceptions

Sikhs believe that God has a personal dimension and that God is saguna (immanent) in everything and everywhere. However, it would be wrong to confuse the Sikh understanding of God with that of any other religious tradition. God is also nirguna (transcendent, or above everything) and, unlike some Hindu conceptions of God, never becomes incarnate. God can be experienced but is beyond human understanding.

Teaching ideas

- Talk to the children about their view of God. Ask them to describe God.
- Look at the words in the Mool Mantra.
- Design a poster with suitable words and symbols to illustrate the Sikh view of God.
- Using a copy of Nit nem, Sikh daily prayers, copy out some of the Sikh prayers and illustrations.
- Discuss and write about how a God-centred life can be different from a self-centred life.

Guru Nanak

Subject facts

His early life

Guru Nanak, the first Sikh Guru, was born on 15 April 1469 in Talwandi, a village in the western Punjab. Stories of Guru Nanak's life are contained in the **Janam Sakhis**. He was born into a Hindu family. His father was an accountant who was employed by the Muslim authorities. It was not surprising therefore that as a child Nanak was friendly with both Hindu and Muslim children. As a child, Nanak was very interested in spiritual matters. He was also bright and studied Hindi and mathematics as well as Muslim literature in Persian and Arabic. Like other Hindu children, when Nanak turned 13 years, he was due to be invested with the sacred thread – a 'coming of age' custom of the Hindu tradition (see point number 10 on page 87). However, to the disappointment of his family, Nanak refused the thread, singing:

Let mercy be the cotton, contentment the thread, continence the knot and truth the twist.

Guru Granth Sahib

This is an early indication of Nanak's future teachings, which say that values and 'truthful living' are more important than religious rituals.

Nanak spent most of his time as a youth discussing spiritual matters with Hindu and Muslim holy men. Thinking that married life might make Nanak concentrate more on everyday concerns, a suitable girl was found for him and he was married at the age of 16. He was happily married and had two children, but was not distracted from his spiritual concerns. He also took a job as an accountant. He would work during the day but at night and in the early mornings he would meditate and sing hymns.

Nanak's call

Early one morning, at the age of 30, accompanied by his musician friend Mardana, Nanak went down to the river to bathe. Tradition tells us that he disappeared from sight for three days. During that time Nanak was in communion with God and was taught the Mool Mantra (see page 175).

All Nanak's friends and family assumed that he had drowned but he reappeared three days later at the spot from which he had disappeared. He was no longer the same person and he shone with a divine light. He seemed to be in a trance and said nothing. He gave up his job and distributed all of his possessions to the poor. When he finally broke his silence he uttered the memorable and famous words, 'There is no Hindu, no Muslim.' When asked by a Muslim to explain this, he said:

Let God's grace be the mosque, and devotion the prayer mat. Let the Qur'an be good conduct.

Guru Granth Sahib

These words are confirmation that Nanak was a teacher in the tradition of the Sants – spiritual teachers who were particularly prominent in northern India in the 15th to 17th centuries. They emphasised a strict and mystical devotion to God, who cannot take human form. Hence all human beings were children of God even though they might follow different religions. What Nanak's teachings gave the Sikh tradition is a belief that it is not important if a person is, say, Sikh, Hindu or Christian. The important thing is to be a good, or true, Sikh, Hindu or Christian.

Mission

After this experience, Nanak, accompanied by Mardana on the rebec (an ancient stringed instrument played with a bow), began travelling all over the Far and Middle East spreading his message.

Nanak's beliefs caused him to be a very courageous person. In his extensive travels he often confronted established beliefs in the name of truth. When travelling in India to the pilgrimage site of Hardwar on the banks of the Ganges, he found a group of devoted Hindus taking ritual baths and offering holy water to the sun. Nanak asked them why they were doing that. They replied that they were offering the water to their ancestors. On hearing this Nanak began throwing water in the opposite direction. When asked what he was doing he told the devotees that he was throwing the water towards his fields because they were dry. They laughed and asked him how he thought the water could reach his fields, which were so far away. He replied that if their water could reach their ancestors, why could it not his reach his fields? The pilgrims saw the folly of their ways and became his devotees.

Nanak also visited Makkah, the holiest city for Muslims and the birthplace of the Prophet Muhammad. He was so tired that he fell asleep with his feet pointing towards the holy **Ka'bah**. When the night watchman noticed this he kicked Nanak's feet and asked how he dared point his feet towards the holy house of God (many religious people do not point their feet towards sacred objects or places as it displays disrespect). Nanak explained he was weary and asked the man kindly to point his feet towards a place where God was not present.

Eventually Nanak returned home and settled down in Kartharpur with his wife and family. Pilgrims came from all directions to listen to his teachings. Nanak believed in a castless society without any distinctions of wealth, birthright, sex or religion. He instigated the communal kitchen called the **langar**. Everyone, kings or homeless people, sits together on the same level to share a common meal. Langar is a fundamental practice for all Sikhs today. Before he died, Nanak appointed **Guru Angad**, one of his most devoted disciples, as his successor.

Nanak's death

In 1539, when Guru Nanak knew he was soon going to die, his Hindu followers said, 'We will cremate you' and his Muslim followers said, 'We will bury you.' Nanak told them to place flowers on either side of him: Hindu to the right, Muslim to the left. He told them that those whose flowers remained fresh could have their way. He lay down and covered himself with a sheet. He died on 22 September 1539. When his followers lifted the sheet they found nothing but the flowers, all still fresh. The Hindus took their flowers and cremated them; the Muslims took theirs and buried them.

Why you need to know these facts

Guru Nanak is the first Sikh Guru. His life and teachings challenged many of the religious beliefs and practices of his time and laid the foundations of the Sikh religion, which lays stress on devotion to God, service to others and the value of family life and hard work. Knowing about the life of Guru Nanak is an essential step towards understanding the Sikh religion. The essence of Sikh teaching is summed up in these words of Guru Nanak:

> *Realisation of Truth is higher than all else. Higher still is truthful living.*

Vocabulary

Guru Angad (1504–52) – the second Guru, ordained by Guru Nanak.
Janam Sakhis –'life story' of Guru Nanak.
Ka'bah – Muslim shrine in Makkah; Muslims believe it to be the first house built for the worship of the One True God.
Langar – Guru's kitchen; the gurdwara dining hall and the food served in it. Everyone, regardless of status, is welcome to stay for langar.

Sikhism

Sensitive issues

- Sikhs are, generally, very open in their faith commitments. Sikhism is not an 'exclusivist' faith but accepts the truth in all traditions.
- When showing images of Guru Nanak in class, it is better to use pictures of him rather than the small plastic statues that are sometimes available. The statues are rather like Hindu murtis (statues of the gods) and, as Nanak didn't accept that such 'icons' were necessary, use of such statues representing Nanak might be rather misleading.

Common misconceptions

Guru Nanak is often referred to as the 'founder' of Sikhism. Whilst some Sikhs would agree with this, there are problems with referring to Nanak as the founder of Sikhism. Firstly, Nanak preached an eternal message, which came from God. In other words, Nanak preached a revealed religion but not one exclusive to the Sikhs. One indication of this is that the Sikh scriptures contain the writings of Hindu and Muslim saints. Secondly, what we now regard as the Sikh identity of the five Ks began with the final Guru, Guru Gobind Singh, and not Guru Nanak.

Teaching ideas

- Watch the *Animated World Faiths* programme (on DVD from Channel 4) about Guru Nanak.
- As a class, discuss Nanak's life. What kind of man do the children think the Guru was?
- Create an illustrated class book about Guru Nanak. Discuss the Guru's teachings, for example equality of all people. Look for examples from Guru Nanak's life.
- Discuss with the children what Guru Nanak would want to change if he were alive today. Use the discussion as a basis for class writing.

The Sikh Gurus

Subject facts

Guru Angad (1504–52)

Angad, originally a Hindu called Lehna, first met Guru Nanak at the age of 27. Up until that point Lehna had been a devotee of the Hindu goddess, Durga. Upon meeting Guru Nanak, Lehna became a devout disciple and, acting on the Guru's instructions, returned home to instruct the local people in the ways of Sikhism. He spent his time praying and serving the people, particularly by distributing food to the poor daily. Eventually he returned to Guru Nanak in Kartharpur, where he became utterly devoted to the service of Nanak. After putting him through a number of 'tests' Guru Nanak changed Lehna's name to Angad (my limb) and appointed him as his successor.

Guru Angad is remembered for consolidating a number of key aspects of the Sikh faith. He popularised the **Gurmukhi** script that was introduced by Guru Nanak. This was a simple written form of Punjabi, which encouraged literacy amongst people of the Punjab. Up to this time the **Brahmins** (high-caste Hindus) had held a monopoly on learning. Guru Angad also started schools for children to learn the Gurmukhi script and so encouraged ordinary people to read sacred literature. He wrote the first biography of Guru Nanak, gathering together some of the first Guru's hymns.

Guru Angad laid stress on the equality of all human beings and extended the practice of langar, which Guru Nanak had initiated to break down barriers of caste. Guru Angad is recorded as saying:

The bodies of men are made from the same five elements, so how can one amongst them be high and the other low?

Guru Angad also took a keen interest in physical fitness and encouraged his devotees to be involved in sports after morning prayers. Today, many gurdwaras organise sporting events.

Guru Amar Das (1479–1574)

Amar Das became the third Guru in 1552, aged 73. He was made Guru because of his selfless service and his great humility and wisdom. A story is told of how Guru Angad's son was angry and kicked Guru Amar Das. Guru Amar Das did not get angry but apologised to the son saying, 'Pardon me; my hard bones must have hurt your foot.'

Guru Amar Das did much to encourage Sikhs in their faith. He appointed a devout Sikh to be in charge of each of the 22 regions of the Punjab. In order to bring Sikhs closer to each other, he gathered them together three times during the year, at the Hindu festival times of **Baisakhi** (April), **Maghi** (mid-January) and **Diwali** (October–November). He also continued the practice of langar, and impressed the Emperor Akbar, who came to pay his respects and to eat with the Sikhs.

Guru Ram Das (1534–81)

Guru Ram Das was installed as Guru at the age of 40. He continued Sikh missionary work, but is best remembered for founding the city of Amritsar in 1574. Many Sikhs settled in Amritsar because it was situated on the trade routes.

He also composed hymns, including the Lawan, a four-stanza hymn that forms a central part of Anand Karaj (the marriage ceremony, see pages 204–5). Shortly before his death, he was succeeded by his son, Arjan.

Guru Arjan (1563–1606)

Guru Arjan became Guru in 1581 just before the death of his father, Guru Ram Das. He became the first Sikh martyr when he was tortured and killed in 1606 on the orders of the Mughal emperor, Jahangir.

He is remembered for a number of significant achievements. He completed the building of the city of Amritsar (in the Punjab province of India) including the **Harmandir Sahib** (the Golden Temple, see page 190). He is also remembered for compiling the Adi Granth (the first version of the Guru Granth Sahib). The Adi Granth included the hymns of the first four Gurus and Guru Arjan's own hymns. The work was completed in 1604 and was installed in the Golden Temple.

Guru Arjan was very popular with the people, but when the Mughal Jahangir succeeded the Emperor Akbar, the Sikhs began to suffer. Jahangir tried to get Guru Arjan to remove some hymns from the Adi Granth and also to become a Muslim. When he refused he was tortured and eventually thrown into a river and killed.

Guru Hargobind (1595–1644)

Guru Hargobind was the son of Guru Arjan and succeeded him in 1606. After his father's torture and murder he realised that the Sikh community and other non-Muslim communities had to defend the right to practise their faith. He organised the Sikhs to defend the weak and helpless. Instead of wearing prayer beads, he took to wearing two kirpans (swords): one was to stand for peeri (spiritual power or God's truth), and the other to stand for meeri (worldly power and the use of physical strength to defend others). These two kirpans now form part of the Sikh symbol called the **khanda** (see page 198).

Guru Har Rai (1630–61)

Guru Har Rai was installed as Guru at the tender age of 14. He is largely remembered for providing free medical aid to the needy. This practice is now a common feature of gurdwaras in India.

Guru Har Krishnan (1656–64)

Guru Har Krishnan was only five years old when he was installed as Guru. He had only been a Guru for three years when he died from smallpox after tending the sick.

Guru Tegh Bahadur (1621–75)

Guru Tegh Bahadur became a Guru in 1664 and was the youngest son of Guru Hargobind. His time as Guru coincided with Mughal persecution of Hindus. Emperor Aurengzeb was forcing Hindus to convert to Islam, killing those who refused. The Hindu Brahmins (the priestly caste) appealed to the Guru to help them. As the Sikh message was concerned with equality and the freedom of people to live their own religion, the Guru and some of his followers agreed. This eventually led to the Guru's imprisonment and death. Guru Tegh Bahadur was the second Sikh martyr.

Guru Gobind Singh (1666–1708)

Guru Gobind Singh, the tenth and final human Guru, succeeded on the death of Guru Tegh Bahadur. He also inherited the situation that had led to the previous Guru's death. The Mughal persecutions continued and Gobind Singh felt the need to organise the Sikhs into a more effective military force. It was at this time that the notion of a Sikh being a soldier saint was born and the **Panj Piare** (the five beloved ones) came into being (see pages 191–2). The Guru also asked all his faithful followers to wear the five Ks (see pages 194–5) as a sign of faithfulness and commitment. He also gave all Sikh males the title of 'singh' (lion), and all female Sikhs the title of 'kaur' (princess).

Before he died, Guru Gobind Singh announced that there would be no more human Gurus and that the Sikh teacher would from thenceforth be the holy scriptures, the Guru Granth Sahib (see pages 188–9).

Why you need to know these facts

It is not necessary to know about the lives and teachings of the other Gurus in enormous detail. Nevertheless, it is important to be aware of their main contributions to the development of the faith. Arjan, Hargobind, Tegh Bahadur and Gobind Singh are particularly important.

Vocabulary

Avatar – the belief that God descends to earth to restore righteousness. Sikhs reject belief in avatars.

Baisakhi – second month of the Hindu calendar; spring harvest festival in the Punjab, celebrated by Sikhs in April to remember the forming of the Khalsa (the community of the pure).

Brahmins – priestly caste of Hinduism.

Diwali – a major Hindu festival celebrated in October–November. In 1577, the foundation stone of the Golden Temple was laid at Diwali, and Guru Harogobind was released from prison at Diwali in 1619.

Gurdwara – 'the doorway to the Guru'; a Sikh temple.
Gurmukhi – 'from the mouth of the Guru'; the written form
of Punjabi used in the Sikh scriptures.
Karma – in Hinduism the law of cause and effect which results
in reincarnation.
Maghi – Hindu month in which the winter solstice falls.

Sensitive issues

Many Sikhs would prefer the Gurus not to be represented
as characters in plays or enactments of ceremonies. You
can use the words of the Gurus if spoken by a third person.
If in doubt about this, contact a Sikh community or an
RE centre.

Common misconceptions

- Sikhs regard the Gurus with great reverence. They believe
them to be divinely inspired – iconography often shows the
Gurus with haloes. Sikhs also believe that the Gurus were
born as spiritually liberated human beings as a result of God's
will (hukam). They were not like ordinary people whose births
are subject to **karma**, the consequences of one's past deeds.
However, the Gurus are not seen as God or **avatars** of God
and are not worshipped. In the Guru Granth Sahib, Guru
Gobind Singh is reported as saying:

> Those who call me Supreme Being shall fall into the pit of hell.
> God neither comes to nor departs from this earth.

- Despite the fact that some Gurus appointed their sons as
successor, the line of Gurus is not a bloodline. The fact that
Guru Nanak gave Lehna the name Angad (my limb) illustrates
that the succession was passed on to those who were deemed
suitable to continue the same message, as originally revealed to
Guru Nanak.

Teaching ideas

- Ask the children to bring in pictures of people who mean a lot to them and ask them to explain why. Get the children to paint pictures of important people in our lives.
- Look at posters of the Gurus. The iconography in the posters often makes the faces look the same, despite differences in beards and so on. This emphasises that each Guru taught the same message. Explore this with the children.
- Explore with the children the kind of commitments they would stand up for. Explore how religious people show commitment to their faith, for example by worship or charitable giving.
- To integrate this work with other aspects of RE or history, explore the importance of people being able to read the scriptures for themselves, as pioneered by Guru Nanak and his immediate successors. Compare this to the development of translated copies of the Bible.

The Guru Granth Sahib

Subject facts

The Guru Granth Sahib is a compilation of 5894 shabads (hymns) composed by six of the Sikh Gurus, plus a large number of hymns written by Hindu and Muslim saints whose views matched those of the Sikhs.

In 1604, Guru Arjan, the fifth Guru, collected together the writings of the first four Gurus and his own and compiled the Adi Granth (first book). This scripture was installed in the Harmandir Sahib (the Golden Temple) in the same year.

In 1706, the tenth Guru, Guru Gobind Singh, added the writings of Guru Tegh Bahadur to the Adi Granth and declared that there would be no more human Gurus – the Adi Granth was to become the Sikhs' living Guru. It became known as the Guru Granth Sahib – *sahib* is an Indian word, used to show respect. Guru Gobind Singh was a wonderful poetic writer himself but did not include any of his writings in the Guru Granth

Sahib. So in 1734, 26 years after his death, a close companion, Bhai Mani Singh, compiled his writings. This compilation became known as the Dasam Granth (collection of the tenth Guru).

The Guru Granth Sahib has 1430 pages. Each copy of it is identical in the way its pages are set out. Therefore a particular hymn in the book always begins at the same place on the same page, no matter where the book is being read. It is written in Gurmukhi, a written form of Punjabi popularised and developed by the second Guru, Angad. 'Gurmukhi' means 'from the Guru's mouth' and Sikhs believe that the scriptures contain the actual words of the Gurus. Gurdwaras will often hold Punjabi lessons for youngsters at the weekend.

The Guru Granth Sahib was copied out by hand until 1852, when the first printed copy appeared. However, no one is allowed to print copies of the book except a special Sikh organisation based in Amritsar. No words can be taken away from the book.

At special times, in all gurdwaras and in the personal and community life of the Sikhs, the Guru Granth Sahib is read straight through in one go. This takes about 48 hours and is called the **Akhand Path**. The reading is shared between a number of people, each person usually reading for two hours at a time. There should be no break in the continuous reading. The readers can be any members of the Sikh community who can read the Guru Granth Sahib accurately.

In the light of all this it is not surprising that the Guru Granth Sahib is treated with the utmost respect. It is treated with the reverence that Sikhs would have shown to the Gurus during their lifetime. It holds the highest authority and Sikhs will prostrate themselves before the book when attending the gurdwara.

Why you need to know these facts

Like many religious scriptures, the Guru Granth Sahib has a position of great authority and plays an enormously important role in the lives of Sikhs. It would be interesting in the context of religious education to look at the Guru Granth Sahib not only as a sacred book treated with enormous respect, but also as a teacher.

Sikhism

Vocabulary

Harmandir Sahib – 'temple of God'; the Sikh temple in Amritsar which is sometimes called Darbar Sahib (Divine Court) and is commonly known as the Golden Temple.

Amazing facts

The Guru Granth Sahib is treated like a living person of great authority. During the night, or after the Akhand Path, it is kept in a special room, rather like a bedroom. This place is sometimes called the Sachkhand (abode of truth). In the morning, the Guru Granth Sahib is taken in procession from its resting place to be ceremonially installed on a platform with a canopy overhead.

Common misconceptions

It is sometimes believed that Sikhs can't have a copy of the Guru Granth Sahib at home. This is not true, but any family wanting to house a copy must have a room for it to 'rest' in and they must be able to treat it with due respect. This means that no person may drink or smoke in the house. Many Sikhs do house a copy of the book. It is true, however, that one cannot just go and buy a copy of Guru Granth Sahib like one can buy a copy of the Qur'an, for instance.

Teaching ideas

- Ask the children to make a collection of books that are special to them and say why their books are special.
- Discuss what people can learn from books.
- Discuss in what ways a book can be like a teacher.
- Discuss the different ways we can show respect.

- Copy out the Punjabi alphabet and get the children to write their names.
- Make a decorated display of some of the hymns of the Guru Granth Sahib.

The Khalsa

Subject facts

The **Khalsa** (the community of the pure), was created by Guru Gobind Singh at Anandpur in the Punjab on Baisakhi day, 30 March 1699. Mughal leaders were constantly threatening Sikhs and so Guru Gobind Singh called his followers together and asked who was strong enough to die for the faith. Five men volunteered and one by one accompanied the Guru into his tent. Each time the Guru reappeared with a bloodstained sword. After the fifth man had volunteered the Guru reappeared with all five, unharmed. They were, however, spiritually transformed by the experience and were given the title Panj Piare (five beloved ones). The five men were 'baptised' by the Guru in a ceremony known as **Amrit Sanskar**. Guru Gobind Singh sprinkled amrit (water with sugar stirred by a khanda – a double-edged sword) over the Panj Piare. The Panj Piare then drank amrit and made vows of commitment to the faith. Afterwards, the five 'baptised' Guru Gobind Singh, and then Guru Gobind Singh 'baptised' many thousands of men and women into the Khalsa.

The Guru conferred the titles 'singh' or 'kaur' on men and women who had joined the Khalsa; this was to signify the Sikh teaching of equality. Amongst Hindus, people's caste could be identified by their name. For Sikhs, their identity was to be derived from their membership of the Khalsa and not from the caste to which they had belonged. Hence the founding of the Khalsa had reinforced the original mission of Guru Nanak. To signify this new identity, Sikhs who had joined the Khalsa began to wear symbolic marks called Panj Kakkar (the five Ks, see page 194) as a symbol of their faith and commitment. They kept the vows they had made during the Amrit Sanskar ceremony. These vows include a commitment to:

- Not eat meat which had been ritually slaughtered.
- Follow the teachings of the Guru and serve the Guru, with arms if necessary.
- Offer daily prayers.
- Give to charity.
- Reject all caste differences.
- Wear the five Ks.
- Not remove hair from the body.
- Not take drugs or intoxicants.
- Respect all women and be faithful in marriage.

Amrit Sanskar today

Today, Sikhs still join the Khalsa through the Amrit Sanskar ceremony. Amrit Sanskar usually takes place in a gurdwara and always takes place in the presence of the Guru Granth Sahib. It is performed by five people who represent the original Panj Piare. These five, those who are taking amrit, and the person who is reading the Guru Granth Sahib are the only ones who are allowed to witness the ceremony.

Water and sugar are put into a steel bowl called a bata. This mixture is stirred by a khanda, as in the original ceremony in 1699. Whilst this is happening, the Panj Piare recite five prayers, including the **japji** of Guru Nanak. The Panj Piare and those taking amrit then kneel on their right knee and raise their left one. This is to symbolise that they are prepared to defend the faith. After the prayers, the candidates drink some amrit from their cupped hands and the amrit is sprinkled five times onto both their eyes and into their hair. Sikhs who have taken amrit must then wear the five Ks.

Why you need to know these facts

The founding of the Khalsa made Sikhs stronger in their identity and it has the same purpose today. The Khalsa is the foundation of modern Sikh identity. It is also an example of how the message of the Sikh Gurus was particularised. The Panj Piare came from different castes and regions but displayed a common commitment to the Sikh faith. The themes of community and identity are central ones for RE and studying the Khalsa can provide many opportunities for exploring these themes with

children, especially in terms of their views about their own
identity and sense of belonging.

Vocabulary

Amrit Sanskar – initiation into the Khalsa.
Japji – the first of Guru Nanak's shabads (hymns). A Sikh should
recite the japji every morning.
Khalsa – the community of the pure; the Sikh community.
Khanda – double-edged sword used to stir amrit; also the symbol
on the Sikh flag.

Sensitive issues

Although the Gurus condemned caste, in practice this message
has not been adopted totally. In some instances, caste manifests
itself in UK gurdwaras where everyone is welcome but one
group dominates the committee.

Amazing facts

Guru Gobind Singh had to fight many battles against the Mughals
to preserve the Sikh community. The Mughals were far greater
in number than the Sikhs. The Guru lost four sons during these
times. Two older sons were killed in battle, while his two younger
sons were 'walled up' (buried) alive for refusing to turn to Islam
as their religion.

Common misconceptions

Not all Sikhs are members of the Khalsa. Visitors to gurdwaras
are sometimes confused when they see men with short hair or
no beards. Such men are still Sikhs, but they may, for instance, just
wear the kara (see page 195). Any person brought up in a Sikh
family is regarded as a Sikh. Initiation into the Khalsa is seen as a

voluntary act and should only be taken by those who understand the significance of it. It is perfectly possible for a man to change his mind and regrow his hair, receive Amrit Sanskar and become a full member of the Khalsa.

Teaching ideas

- Get the children to write a story about a time they had to stand up for something they believed in.
- Get the children to write about something that they would be prepared to stand up for.
- Ask the children to write a set of rules that a group of friends might obey.

The five Ks

Subject facts

The Panj Kakkar (five Ks) are very important Sikh symbols. All 'baptised' Sikhs, both men and women, wear the symbols of the five Ks. They link Sikhs to the origins of their faith as well as reminding them of key Sikh teachings.

The five Ks are:

> **Kesh** – uncut hair
> **Kanga** – a small wooden comb
> **Kara** – a steel bracelet
> **Kirpan** – a small sword
> **Kachera** – underwear

Kesh – uncut hair

This is a symbol of Sikh spirituality as many holy men in history have worn uncut hair. It also represents 'cosmic man' to Sikhs; this emphasises humankind's connection to God's intentions at Creation when human beings were formed from the earth. The kesh also represents freedom from tribalism and divisions amongst human beings – people have traditionally shown their loyalties through different headdresses. Not cutting one's hair applies to the whole body and not just the head.

Kanga – a small wooden comb

The kanga is used to keep the hair clean and free from being matted. The kanga therefore symbolizes the discipline needed to keep the faith. Also, in Indian religious tradition, matted hair symbolises world renunciation so it is important for Sikhs to keep their hair clean and free from the matted condition.

Kara – a steel bracelet

This circular bracelet represents the circle of life. As in all Indian religions, a wheel symbolises the eternal round of births and rebirths. The kara also stands for submission to the 'eternal way'; like the kara, God has no beginning and no end. For many Sikhs, the kara also acts as a conscience – worn on their wrist it reminds Sikhs of their Khalsa vows if they are about to do something wrong. Some describe it as half a handcuff, the other half being attached to God.

Kirpan - a small sword

The kirpan is sometimes referred to as the 'sword of mercy' and represents defence of all. It symbolises the defence of all people against tyranny. It should only be used in extreme circumstances and should only be used as an offensive weapon to uphold righteousness. Spiritually, the kirpan is a symbolic weapon that cuts through **avidya** (ignorance) and therefore represents God – it is God who ultimately destroys human ignorance or spiritual blindness.

Kachera – underwear

Traditionally, Sikhs wore white shorts called kachera when going into battle. They were far more practical than the traditional Indian **dhoti**. Spiritually speaking, the kachera represent control of lust – one of the five impulses according to Sikhism. They don't stand for chastity, as Sikhs believe this to be unnatural, but they do stand for faithfulness and fidelity in sexual relationships.

Why you need to know these facts

The five Ks are the most visible symbol of Sikhism. However, they are not just a uniform. They are hugely important symbols that remind Sikhs of various spiritual teachings and are seen as a concrete aid to living a truly Sikh lifestyle.

In the context of religious education, an exploration of the five Ks could centre on the idea of identity and lifestyle. Ask the children to give you examples of anything they wear or do that identifies them, for example club badges or school uniform.

Vocabulary

Avidya – spiritual ignorance.
Dhoti – a piece of cloth wrapped around the loins. A traditional form of dress amongst Hindu men.

Sensitive issues

● Be careful when handling the five Ks, in particular the kirpan, which should not be drawn from its sheath, as it is not a weapon of aggression. Also be sensitive when showing children the kachera. Because this is a 'one size' Indian garment held up by a draw-string, it can be seen as a bit of a joke by children who are not used to such garments.
● Be sensitive if you have Sikh children in your class who might be wearing the kara. This can be seen as dangerous in PE, for example. However, it is never fair nor wise to ask for it to be removed. In Birmingham, children will cover the kara with a sweatband to make it safer to wear.

Amazing facts

When Sikhs first began to settle in the UK, many Sikh men cut their hair to avoid prejudice and to enable them to get a job. Happily, nowadays most Sikh men are proud to wear all five Ks, as Britain has become a more aware and understanding society.

Common misconceptions

● It is often assumed that the turban is one of the five Ks. It is not. The hair is the symbol; the turban is worn to keep the hair tidy.
● It is not just men who wear the five Ks. Women wear them also.

Teaching ideas

● Get the children to talk about and bring into school examples of clothes, badges or any other symbols that indicate that they belong to an organisation. Investigate with the children the meanings behind uniforms, badges and so on. Get the children to write down any rules that go with membership.
● Get the children to discuss why they think some Sikhs cut their hair and do not wear the five Ks.
● Bring in real examples of the five Ks and produce a wall chart that illustrates them and explains their spiritual meanings.

The gurdwara

Subject facts

The word 'gurdwara' means 'the doorway to the Guru'. Gurdwaras can be beautiful buildings like the Golden Temple (see page 190), but they can also be a humble house. Any place where the Guru Granth Sahib is kept becomes a gurdwara.

Some gurdwaras in Britain are purpose-built, with beautiful domes. Others are converted churches and cinemas. Outside all of them flies the Sikh flag, the **Nishan Sahib** (see Figure 7). On this saffron-coloured flag is the khanda. This symbol gets its name from the double-edged sword that stands for Divine Knowledge – the knowledge that can cleave truth from falsehood. The circle around the khanda is called the chakar and symbolizes the eternal nature of God and the oneness and equality of humanity. The chakar is surrounded by two kirpans and symbolizes the twin concepts of peeri and meeri (see page 185), which stand for spiritual power and temporal authority, and emphasise that a Sikh should remember God but also contribute to society.

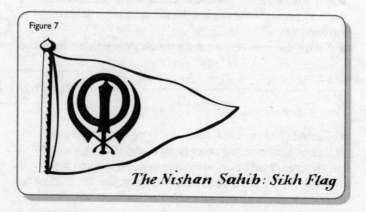

Figure 7

The Nishan Sahib: Sikh Flag

Worship

All gurdwaras have a room where the Guru Granth Sahib is read and people meet for worship. The continuous reading of the scriptures, called Akhand Path (see page 209), is a permanent feature of Sikh worship in larger gurdwaras. In smaller gurdwaras, the Akhand Path may take place at weekends. It always takes place at gurpurbs (religious anniversaries, see pages 207–8). Sikh families also arrange for Akhand Path to take place to mark special times, such as births, marriages and deaths (see pages 204–5).

Sikhs and anyone else who wants to worship God can visit the gurdwara. Some gurdwaras are open 24 hours a day; others have more limited hours. People can come into the gurdwara to pray and listen to the Akhand Path. Prayers are said in the gurdwara every morning and evening. Afterwards, the worshippers can stay to eat langar, a meal served by volunteers from the congregation. The word 'langar' refers to both the meal and the room or dining hall in which it is served. This practice of serving langar was begun by Guru Nanak (see page 180).

Sikhs do not have a special day of the week for worship; every day is sacred. Nevertheless, in Britain, most Sikhs attend services on Saturday or Sunday. A service at the weekend can last for five or six hours and include a meal in the langar. During the service, the congregation perform kirtan: devotional singing of shabads from the Guru Granth Sahib to music played on tabla (drums) and a harmonium. Any person can perform kirtan but usually it is the ragees (professional musicians) who play and sing. Next, Anand Sahib, a hymn composed by Guru Amar Das, is recited. Afterwards, the congregation stands for a prayer called the **ardas**. The congregation sits down and the **granthi** (reader of the Guru Granth Sahib) opens the Guru Granth Sahib at random and reads a shabad from that page. This is called the hukam (message for the day). During the service, karah prashad (blessed food) is distributed to everyone present. The worshippers stay for langar afterwards.

Why you need to know these facts

The gurdwara is an excellent example of Sikhs living in community. Two important Sikh words for this are satsang (congregation) and panth (used by Sikhs to describe their community; so the Sikh Panth). The concept of community provides a rich theme for religious education and it is a good idea to point out to children the aspects of community that can be learned from study of or visit to a gurdwara.

Vocabulary

Ardas – formal prayer that begins or ends every ritual. Its three parts encourage Sikhs to remember the Gurus, the teachings of the Guru Granth Sahib and to ask for God's blessing on the Sikh community and all peoples.

Granthi – one who reads the Guru Granth Sahib. There is no priesthood in Sikhism. Although any member of the congregation can read from the book, the granthi plays a special role in caring for the Guru Granth Sahib.

Sensitive issues

- Take off your shoes when entering a gurdwara.
- When entering the prayer hall you will probably be expected to pay respects to the Guru Granth Sahib.
- Try not to turn your back or point your feet at the scriptures.
- Tobacco and alcohol are not allowed into the gurdwara.
- Visitors should keep their heads covered.
- It is common practice for men and women to sit separately in the prayer hall. However, this is a cultural custom and if you visit a gurdwara on a day when it is not very busy it is quite likely that you will be able to sit in a group without segregation.

Amazing facts

- The first gurdwara in the UK was opened in Shepherd's Bush in London in 1911, even though most Sikhs didn't come to the UK until the 1960s and 1970s.
- About 56 per cent of the Sikhs in Britain were born here.

Common misconceptions

The gurdwara is often referred to as a Sikh temple, but this suggests that it is the building that matters. What is important is the concept that a Sikh is entering a place where a Guru will be found. In this sense the Guru is the Guru Granth Sahib, and this is what makes it a gurdwara.

Teaching ideas

- Make two lists of words, one to describe a house and one to describe a home. Talk about the differences. Discuss aspects of a gurdwara that make it seem like a home.
- Prepare some langar food: chapatti, dal, vegetable curry and yoghurt. Invite the school to join you in eating together.
- Discuss the word 'hospitality' with the children. Ask them to draw up some rules for welcoming visitors into school.

Sikh values and family life

Subject facts

The Gurus taught that family life is very important and that marriage is essential to maintain family life. In the Hindu tradition, spiritual development follows four stages of life, called ashramas (see pages 80–1), the final stage being sannyasin (world renunciation). Sikhism rejects world renunciation and recognises only the second ashrama, grihasta, that of 'householder'. Sikh spirituality emphasises living in the world and believes that the responsibilities of marriage bring a spiritual balance to one's life. Sikhs therefore balance worship and meditation with **kirat karna** (honest work) and sewa (service to others).

Sikhs believe they can only achieve spiritual liberation when they overcome a self-centred and materialistic view of the world. Humans suffer from haumai, which gives rise to the five vices: lust, anger, greed, worldly attachment and pride. By being happily married and practising the three virtues of nam simran (keeping God constantly in mind), kirat karna and **vand chhakna**, a Sikh can develop contentment, charity, kindness, happiness and humility.

Guru Nanak said:

Wandering ascetics, warriors, celibates, sannyasins, none of them obtains the fruit of liberation without performing sewa.

Sikhs believe in the value of all work. Often jobs like cleaning people's shoes in the gurdwara or washing dishes may seem very menial, however they remind Sikhs of humility. Sikhs believe this is an antidote to self-centredness, a major impediment to spiritual happiness. Sikhs should try to earn their living by honest means. They should work hard and only take what they need for themselves and should practise vand chhakna (sharing their wealth for the benefit of the community).

Vand chhakna may mean giving money or time, or using one's skills to help others. It involves helping everyone, not only other Sikhs. Sikhs may share 'themselves' by welcoming visitors to the gurdwara. Gurdwaras in India often open their doors several times a day to provide langar for the poor. For many Sikhs, from an early age, preparing and serving langar are important experiences from which they can learn about sewa. Sikhs might give by providing accommodation for homeless people. However, it would not be possible for somebody to rely on this as it would not aid them spiritually. It is important to be able to stand on your 'own two feet' and make a contribution to the world.

Why you need to know these facts

A study of the spirituality and values of a religion lies at the heart of good RE teaching. There is plenty of opportunity here to talk about the value of family life and acting to do good in the world.

Vocabulary

Halal – meat that is killed and prepared in a way required by Muslims.
Kirat karna – earning one's living by honest means.
Vand chhakna – sharing one's time, talents and earnings with those less fortunate.

Sensitive issues

As always be careful not to make children feel excluded if they don't live in a conventional, two-parent family.

Amazing facts

The story of Lalo and Bhago.

On one of his journeys, Guru Nanak stayed with a carpenter in a place called Emnabad. The carpenter's name was Lalo. A local wealthy man called Bhago decided to give a feast and invited all around including Guru Nanak. However the Guru did not attend and, when asked why, Nanak replied that he would rather eat the carpenter's bread because it had been earned by honest work, whereas Bhago's great feast had been the result of exploitation of the poor. Nanak said that the bread had been stained by the blood of the poor. When Bhago protested, Guru Nanak took a piece of Lalo's bread and a piece of Bhago's bread and squeezed them both. Milk dripped from Lalo's bread whilst Bhago's dripped with blood. Bhago then repented and devoted the rest of his life to those in need.

Common misconceptions

Are Sikhs vegetarian? All food served in the langar is vegetarian and, generally, many Sikhs follow a vegetarian diet. However, Sikhs are not forbidden to eat meat; only **halal** meat is forbidden. Some Sikhs eat meat occasionally at festival times.

Teaching ideas

- Talk about what makes a good person. Make a list of good qualities.
- Discuss ways in which people try to keep God constantly in mind.

- Explore ideas about how the class or school can practise vand chhakna and sewa. Arrange a class or school collection for a good cause.
- Write about 'My family', listing the good things about being a member of a family.

Life ceremonies

Subject facts

There are four ceremonies that mark important times in the life of a Sikh: the naming ceremony, intiation into the Khalsa (Amrit Sanskar), marriage and death. All Sikh ceremonies are held in the presence of the Guru Granth Sahib.

The naming ceremony

A baby, seen as a gift from God, is named a few weeks after the birth. The naming ceremony is often included as part of a normal service in the gurdwara, or it can be held separately either in the gurdwara or at the family's home. After prayers, the child's name is taken from the first letter of the vak (a passage in the Guru Granth Sahib which is read after opening the book at random). A girl's name is followed by 'kaur' and a boy's by 'singh' as instituted by Guru Gobind Singh (page 186).

Marriage – Anand Karaj

Marriage in Sikhism is seen as a spiritual state and not just a social contract. This is because the Gurus proclaimed marriage as the ideal state for spiritual development. The love between wife and husband is compared with the love and longing of the human soul for God. Guru Ram Das composed the marriage hymn (the **Lavan**) in which he said that awe, love, restraint and harmony are as important for the relationship in marriage as they are in the relationship between a devotee and God. Most Sikh marriages are assisted marriages – parents introduce the boy and the girl. A Sikh marriage is seen as a joining of two families, so parents are always involved, although a marriage cannot take place unless both the boy and the girl agree to it.

The Sikh marriage ceremony, **Anand Karaj** (ceremony of bliss) takes place in the presence of the Guru Granth Sahib. The groom, usually wearing a red turban, sits in front of the scripture. Then the bride, also wearing red, sits down by his side with a female companion. A prayer is said and the couple is reminded of their duties to one another. They nod to say they will fulfil their marital duties. At the end, the groom's scarf is placed in the bride's hand. Then the four verses of the Lavan are read. At the end of each verse the couple walk around the Guru Granth Sahib in a clockwise direction, while the ragees (musicians) sing the verse that has just been read. The groom leads the bride and she holds his scarf. After the fourth circling of the scriptures the couple are married. The marriage ceremony ends with the ardas (page 199).

Death

Sikhs believe that death is according to God's will. They see death as a natural part of life and seek solace in reading the Guru Granth Sahib. The scriptures say, 'The dawn of a new day is the message of a sunset. Earth is not your permanent home.'

Sikhs believe in reincarnation. This is often likened to going to sleep at the end of the day and waking up the next morning. Whilst it is recognised that loved ones will feel grief and sorrow, Sikhs are encouraged to remember that the person who has died has gone on to another life. Before they go to sleep, Sikhs read **Kirtan Sohila**, which is also the prayer used at funerals.

Sikhs normally cremate their dead. Before the funeral, the body is washed and, if the person had been initiated into the Khalsa (pages 191–2), dressed in the five Ks (page 194). The body is taken to a crematorium in a procession. At the crematorium the granthi (page 200) leads the mourners in the Kirtan Sohila. The mourners are reminded of the aim of life, which is:

Know the real purpose of being here, gather up treasure under the guidance of the **Sat Guru***. Make your mind God's home. If God abides with you undisturbed you will not be reborn.*

Finally, the ardas is said to ask for peace for the dead person's soul. The ashes of the dead are usually put into a river or stream. Some Sikhs in Britain take the ashes to scatter in the Punjab.

Sikhism does not allow for the erection of headstones or other memorials. Sikhs believe that the presence of headstones could direct people's worship away from the true God.

Why you need to know these facts

Teaching children about the four key Sikh ceremonies will enable them to gain understanding of essential Sikh values, Sikh identity and Amrit Sanskar, and beliefs about God and the meaning of life. This will enable them to compare Sikh values with key values from other religious traditions.

Vocabulary

Anand Karaj – the marriage ceremony.
Kirtan Sohila – evening prayer; also read at funerals and when the Guru Granth Sahib is laid to rest.
Lavan – marriage hymn composed by Guru Ram Das.
Sat Guru – one true Guru.

Sensitive issues

Ideas about marriage and death can prove to be sensitive issues with some children. While questions about relationships and death lie at the heart of relevant and challenging RE, it is best to be confident that such issues can be handled effectively. It is important to explore the questions as well as the ceremonies.

Common misconceptions

For Sikhs, marriages are traditionally arranged, but the couple are not forced into marrying. Sikhs believe that the couple should come from similar backgrounds. That way, it is believed, the marriage will last and become strong.

Sikhs do not believe that human effort alone can guarantee spiritual liberation. The Guru Granth Sahib says that:

Good actions may procure a better life, but liberation comes only through grace… It is by dwelling on God's Name that one avoids going to hell.

- Talk with the children about their names. Find out their origins and what they mean. Do they have a family name?
- Get the children to choose a new name for themselves by opening a book at random, similar to the practice of vak.
- Discuss why people choose to get married. What are the good and bad things about it? Get the children to produce a wedding invitation and include some Sikh symbols and words from the Lavan.
- Discuss what the children believe happens when we die. Discuss ways in which a person's life can be remembered.

Sikh festivals

Subject facts

There are two types of Sikh festival: the gurpurbs, which are holy days in honour of a Guru, and melas (literally, 'fair'), which are important Sikh celebrations that coincide with Hindu festivals.

The celebration of all the festivals includes the Akhand Path. The 48-hour reading is timed to finish on the morning of the festival day. Hymns are sung and lectures are given on the significance of the day. Kara prashad (a sweet vegetarian pudding representing a blessing from the Guru) is distributed and food is served in the langar hall throughout. Sometimes there are street processions and banners outside the gurdwara.

Gurpurbs – Gurpurbs celebrate events in the lives of the Gurus. The most important ones are:
- The martyrdom of Guru Arjan, celebrated May–June.
- The birthday of Guru Nanak, celebrated Oct–Nov.
- The martyrdom of Guru Tegh Bahadur, celebrated Nov–Dec.
- The birthday of Guru Gobind Singh, celebrated Dec–Jan.

A central feature of the two birthday celebrations is the procession through the streets led by five people who represent the Panj Piare. A decorated float carrying the Guru Granth Sahib follows the procession. Large crowds follow the float singing hymns written by the Guru whose birthday they are celebrating.

Melas – Sikh festivals originated with Guru Amar Das, who commanded his followers to meet together at the Hindu festival times of Baisakhi, Diwali and Maghi. Maghi, the Hindu festival dedicated to Shiva, has been replaced in the Sikh calendar by Hola Mohalla (celebrated at the time of the Hindu festival of Holi). It is believed the intention behind these assemblies was that Guru Amar Das wanted Sikhs to choose where they belonged, in their Hindu culture and background or with the Guru. The two most widely celebrated festivals are Baisakhi and Diwali.

Baisakhi – celebrates the founding of the Khalsa by Guru Gobind Singh in 1699. The festival is usually celebrated on 13 April. In large cities like Birmingham there are huge processions and celebrations, including Bhangra dancing. A central part of the celebrations is the renewal of the Nishan Sahib. The flag and the saffron-coloured cloth that is wrapped around the flagpole are taken down and the flagpole is washed in yoghurt to symbolise purity. The flagpole is then dressed in new cloth and a new flag.

Diwali – during this festival Sikhs commemorate Guru Hargobind's release from prison. In 1619 the Mughal Emperor Jehangir imprisoned the Guru in Gwalior. The charges were found to be false and he was released at Diwali. The Guru refused unless those imprisoned with him were set free. The Emperor agreed to set free as many as could hold on to the Guru's cloak as they left. Because the Guru had a very long cloak all 52 prisoners were released. When the Guru arrived back in Amritsar, the Harmandir Sahib (the Golden Temple) was decorated with lamps. Today, the Golden Temple is illuminated by lights and clay lamps (devas). In the UK, Sikhs burn lamps outside gurdwaras and in the windows of their homes.

Why you need to know these facts

 It is always important to teach about religious festivals and holy days. They lie at the heart of the religion and religious identity. The special days referred to in this section remind Sikhs of key people and events in the development of their faith.

Vocabulary

Akhand Path – continuous reading of the Guru Granth Sahib from beginning to end.
Nishan Sahib – the Sikh flag flown outside a gurdwara.
Panj Piare – 'the five beloved ones'; the first Sikhs to be initiated into the Khalsa; also refers to representatives of these first five who perform the initiation today.

Teaching ideas

- Talk with younger children about birthdays and how they are celebrated. Tell some stories about the birth and childhood of Guru Nanak. Watch the DVD on Guru Nanak from the series *Animated World Faiths* (Channel 4).
- Divide the class into groups to research in more detail each of the gurpurbs and melas. Hold a presentation of their work.
- Get the children to make an attractive calendar showing the main Sikh festivals. Ask them to design a greetings card or invitation for a gurpurb or mela.

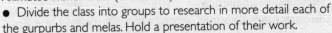

Resources

An excellent introduction to Guru Nanak can be found in *A Gift to the Child* by M. Grimmitt, J. Grove, J. Hull and L. Spencer (Stanley Thornes Ltd). Good Sikh suppliers are *DTF* Publishers and Distributors: **www.dtfbooks.com.**
Artefacts suppliers – Religion in Evidence; Articles of Faith (see page 33); Gohil Emporium (see page 102 for details).
TV programmes – *Animated World Faiths* series for ages 7–11. *Stop, Look, Listen*, 'Water, Moon, Candle, Tree and Sword'. Suitable for KS1 children. Both from Channel 4.
Useful books – *Religion in Focus: Sikhism* by Geoff Teece (Franklin Watts, 2008).
Useful websites – www.sikhs.org; www.reonline.org.uk; http://retoday.org.uk

Glossary

Annica – impermanence.

Bhikkhus – Buddhist monks.

Bhikkunis – Buddhist nuns.

Bodhi tree – the tree under which Buddha attained enlightenment. *Bodhi* means 'enlightenment'.

Dana – generosity, giving.

Dhamma – universal law or eternal truth for Buddhists, the teachings that had remained hidden for years and that Buddha 'uncovered' and passed on.

Dhammachakra – a wheel symbol, with eight spokes representing the Eightfold Path of Bhuddism; like the dhamma – the 'eternal truth' – the wheel has neither a beginning nor end.

Dukkha – suffering, unsatisfactoriness. According to Buddhism the basic disease of human nature from which humans need to be liberated.

Eightfold Path – guiding principles for the practice of Buddhism, with three aspects: wisdom, ethics and mental effort.

Gaya – a town in North-East India. Nearby is Bodh Gaya, which marks the place where Buddha became enlightened. It is now a place of pilgrimage for Buddhists.

Hanamatsuri – a flower festival celebrated in April by Mahayana Buddhists to remember Buddha's birth in the garden at Lumbini, during which an infant Buddha image is bathed and placed in a floral shrine.

Jataka tales – 'birth story' tales; tales of the former lives of Buddha.

Kamma – action; intentional actions that affect one's circumstances in this and future lives.

Kathina Day – a festival celebrated in October by Theravada Buddhists when the lay members of the Buddhist community offer new robes to the monks.

Lotus plant – a traditional Indian symbol of enlightenment.

Metta – loving kindness; love that is not possessive.

Murtis – the images of the Hindu deities, which are the focus of worship. The word 'murti' means 'form'.

Nibbana – 'blowing out' of human desire and delusion; a state of purity and non-attachment to the 'three poisons', ignorance, hatred and greed.

Pagoda – a shrine or memorial building. Pagoda originate with stupas, which were burial mounds covered by a dome in which relics of Buddha are placed.

Pali Canon – the earliest and most complete form of Buddhist scriptures; also called the 'three baskets'.

Parinibbana – a festival celebrated in February by Mahayana Buddhists to remember the death of Buddha.

Samsara – the continual round of birth, sickness, old age and death.

Sangha – the Buddhist community. One of the Three Jewels of Buddhism.

Sarnath – the deer park six miles outside the holy city of Varanasi, India, where Buddha preached his first sermon.

Tanha – desire or craving. The cause of suffering.

Varanasi – holy Hindu city on the River Ganges.

Vihara – dwelling place; a monastery.

Vinaya – the rules of discipline of monastic life.

Wesak – Buddha Day; a celebration of the birth, life, teachings and death of Buddha.

Christianity

Anglican – Churches in full communion with the see of Canterbury. Their origins and traditions are linked to the Church of England.

Apostle – one who was sent by Jesus to preach the Gospel.

Apostolic Succession – the historical link between the Church and the first followers of Jesus.

Atonement – reconciliation between God and humanity; restoring the relationship broken by sin. Sinners are therefore made 'at one' with God through the life, death and resurrection of Jesus.

Chalice – goblet for holding the communion wine.

Glossary

Christ – the 'anointed one'; the Messiah; one of the titles given to Jesus by his followers.

Ecumenism – all efforts to stress those things which all Christians have in common and play down divisions.

Evangelical Church – group or church placing particular emphasis on the Gospel and the scriptures as the sole authority in all matters of faith and conduct.

Font – receptacle to hold water used in baptism.

Fundamentalism – a strictly literalist view of the Bible.

Gospel – 'good news' of salvation in Jesus Christ; the part of the Bible that is an account of Jesus' life and work.

Holy Spirit – the third aspect of God in the Holy Trinity. Active as a divine presence and power in the world and in dwelling in believers to make them like Christ and empower them to do God's will.

Iconostasis – a screen covered with icons used in Eastern Orthodox churches to separate the sanctuary (the part of the church that contains the altar, which is where the bread and wine are consecrated) from the nave (the main body of the church where the worshippers stand).

Icons – paintings or mosaics of Jesus Christ, the Virgin Mary, saints or Church feasts. Used as an aid to worship and devotion, usually in the Orthodox tradition.

Incarnation – the doctrine that God took human form in Jesus Christ. It is also the belief that God in Christ is active in the Church and in the world.

Liturgy – a service of worship, for example Eucharist or Evensong, that follows prescribed rituals. Used in the Orthodox Church for Eucharist.

Lord – title used for Jesus to express his divine lordship over people, time and space.

Mass – term used by Roman Catholics and others for the Eucharist.

Messiah – used in the Jewish tradition to refer to the expected leader who will bring the Jewish people to salvation. Jesus' followers used this title to refer to him.

Missal – the book containing words and ceremonial directions for saying Mass.

Monotheism – belief in only one God.

Nicene Creed – a formal statement of Christian belief based on the creed of the first Council of Nicaea in 325. The creed is recited during the Eucharist service in Orthodox, Roman

Catholic and many Protestant churches.

Paschal candle – a large, special candle associated with Easter. In many Orthodox, Roman Catholic and Anglican churches, a fire is lit on Easter Eve and a new Paschal candle is lit from this fire. The candle is carried through the church, representing the light of Christ who, by his resurrection, conquered the powers of darkness and death.

Pentecostal Church – the branch of the Church that emphasises certain gifts that were given to the first believers on the Day of Pentecost (for example, to heal the sick and speak in tongues).

Protestant – the part of the Church that became distinct from the Roman Catholic and Orthodox traditions when their members professed or protested the centrality of the Bible and other beliefs. Protestants profess that the Bible under the guidance of the Holy Spirit is the ultimate authority for Christian teaching.

Sacrament – an outward sign of an inward blessing. There are seven sacraments; the two most important are baptism and Eucharist.

Salvation – the process of being saved by Christ. Christians view the present human condition as being distorted and believe that it can only be transformed by the saving power of Jesus.

Sin – an act of rebellion or disobedience against God. The human condition in need of transformation.

Stewardship – the belief that God has chosen humanity to be his servants and vice-regents with responsibility for the world.

Traditionalism – the belief that the traditions of the past (the 'deposit of faith') should be kept intact, and all efforts to reformulate or update the faith are detrimental to Christianity.

Trinity – God in three persons: God the Father, God the Son (Jesus Christ) and God the Spirit (the Holy Spirit).

Hinduism

Aarti – a ceremony in which light is offered to the deities and then offered to the devotees.

Ahimsa – reverence for all living things; not killing; non-violence; respect for life. A key Hindu value practised especially by Jains.

Amrit – holy water.

Artha – earning one's living by honest means. One of the four aims of life for Hindus.

Glossary

Atman – the real self, the soul, the divine spark of Brahman within all people.

Aum – a sacred symbol representing the sound of the ultimate reality.

Avatar – 'one who descends'; in this context this refers to manifestations of Vishnu, the two most important being Rama and Krishna.

Ayodhya – town in northern India believed to be the birthplace of Rama, and therefore a place of pilgrimage.

Bhakti yoga – the spiritual path of devotion.

Brahmins – priestly caste of Hinduism.

Darshan – a glimpse of a deity.

Dharma – religious duty of Hindu, based on the person's stage in life and social position.

Dhoti – a piece of cloth wrapped around the loins. A traditional form of dress amongst Hindu men.

Diwali – A major Hindu festival celebrated in October/November.

Ganga Ma – the Mother Goddess; the holy River Ganges.

Ghat – In India, a flight of steps leading down to a river or landing place. On the Ganges at Varanasi one of these ghats is used for funerals, hence the term 'funeral ghat'.

Guru – spiritual teacher; one who leads from darkness to light.

Jainism – an Indian religious movement whose key figure was Mahavira (599–527BCE) the last of the Jain tirthankaras (ford makers) who taught the way to liberation from physical bondage to the world.

Kama – enjoying life's pleasures. One of the four aims in life for Hindus.

Kanyadaan – a ceremony in which the bride is given away during the marriage ceremony.

Karma – the law of cause and effect.

Kumbha Mela – the largest and most important Hindu pilgrimage festival, held every 12 years.

Lingum – representation of Shiva; sometimes referred to as phallic.

Mahabharata – scripture that includes the Bhagavad Gita.

Mantra – that which delivers the mind; a word, a short sacred text or a prayer that is said repetitiously.

Moksha – liberation, freedom from the wheel of samsara.

Murti – 'form'; the image of a deity used in worship.

Prasad – blessed food.

Puja – worship.

Puranas – part of the smriti scriptures; contains many well-known Hindu stories.

Ramayana – Hindu epic relating the story of Rama and Sita.

Samsara – the world, the wearisome wheel, the place through which the soul passes in a series of rebirths.

Sanatan Dharma – 'the eternal way'; most Hindus prefer this title for their religion.

Sannyasin – a world renouncer; a person in the fourth stage of life.

Saptapadi – a ceremony in which the married couple take seven steps together.

Shaivite – devotee of Shiva.

Shakti – feminine divine energy or power.

Shruti – revealed truths; refers particularly to the Vedas.

Smriti – remembered truths; applied to epics such as the Mahabharata and Ramayana.

Tirtha – a place of pilgrimage.

Upanishads – sacred texts that explain the meaning of the Vedas.

Vaishnavite – devotee of Vishnu.

Vedas – from *veda* (knowledge); the four texts believed by Hindus to be revealed scriptures or shruti.

Yoga – spiritual path.

Yogi – someone who meditates; a contemplative who follows the jnana yoga of spiritual insight.

Yuga – age; extended period of time. There are four yugas.

Islam

Adhan – the call to prayer.

Alhamdulillah – 'all praise be to Allah.'

Anbiya (singular nabi) – prophets; to be distinguished from rasul (messenger).

Aqamah – the call to begin prayer.

Bismillah al Rahman al Rahim – 'In the name of God, the Merciful, the Compassionate'; the preface to all surahs of the Qur'an except the ninth.

Din – obedience; submission; religion; Islam (submission to God) is regarded in the Qur'an as al-din (the religion).

Fatihah – the opening surah of the Qur'an:

Glossary

In the name of God, Most Gracious, Most Merciful. Praise be to God, The Cherisher and Sustainer of the Worlds; Most Gracious, Most Merciful; Master of the Day of Judgement.

Hadith – a tradition or narration relating or describing a saying or an action of the Prophet.

Hajj – pilgrimage to Makkah, a male who has performed the hajj is called hajji, a female hajja.

Ibadah – worship.

Id ul-Fitr – festival that breaks the fast of Ramadan, and beginning a day after Ramadan ends. It is also the first day of Shawal, the tenth Islamic month.

Iftar – breaking of the fast each day during Ramadan.

Ihram – the state entered into when performing hajj or umrah (pilgrimage to Makkah at any time during the year). It also refers to the two pieces of white cloth worn by men and the white, modest clothing worn by women.

Ihsan – spirituality.

Imam – leader of congregational prayers.

I'tikaf – special study of the Qur'an during Ramadan.

Jihad – struggle, both physical and moral.

Ka'bah – the shrine in the Grand Mosque in Makkah, said to have been built by Adam and rebuilt by Ibrahim.

Kosher – 'proper'; describes food fit to eat according to Jewish dietry laws.

Muezzin – a man who calls Muslims to prayer.

Mujahid – one who 'fights' in the path of Allah.

Niyyah – right intention.

Qadar – Allah's complete and final control over the fulfilment of events or destiny.

Qiblah – the direction in which Muslims face when praying.

Rahman – God the merciful.

Rak'ah – fixed set of actions performed during salah.

Ramadan – the ninth month of the Muslim calendar; the month of fasting.

Rasul – messenger of Allah.

Sadaqat ul-fitr – voluntary charitable payment.

Salah – the five set, daily prayers.

Sawm – fasting.

Shaytan – rebellious or proud; the devil.

Shi'a or **Shi'ites** – members of a branch of Islam that separated from the orthodox Sunnis in 679CE due to differences about the succession after the death of the Prophet Muhammad. They constitute about 15 per cent of the world's Islamic population.

Subhah – prayer beads used to count recitations of the names of God.

Sufi – a Muslim mystic.

Sunnah – a tradition or custom founded on the example of the Prophet Muhammad.

Tariqah – the 'inward' path of Muslim spirituality, leading to fana or 'self-noughting'. Traditionally an aspect of the Sufi or mystical tradition.

Tawaf – walking seven times around the Ka'bah in worship of Allah.

Wudu – ritual purification; ablutions performed before salah.

Zakah – purification by wealth; an obligatory act of worship in which a devotee gives money to charity.

Zamzam – the well next to the Ka'bah; the place where, according to Muslim belief, water sprang forth for Hagar in answer to her prayers.

Judaism

Aron Hakodesh – Holy Ark; the cupboard in the eastern wall of a synagogue in which the Torah scrolls are kept.

Bimah – desk from where the Torah is read.

Challah – loaves used on Shabbat and festivals.

Covenant – an agreement made between God and humanity when, in return for God's blessing, humanity agrees to keep God's laws.

Haftarah – completion; the portion from the writings of the prophets which is read in the synagogue on Shabbat, after the reading of the Torah.

Hagaddah – retelling; a book used in retelling the Exodus story at the Seder meal on the first evening of the Pesach festival.

Halakhah – 'the way'; the legal teachings of traditional Judaism.

Hanukkah – holiday celebrating the rededication of the Temple during the time of the Maccabbees in 165BC; usually occurs in December.

Hasidic – 'pious one'; a sect of Judaism, founded in the 18th century in Eastern Europe. Hasidic Judaism tends to emphasise mystical experience above study of the Torah and hence is rejected by some Orthodox groups.

Glossary

Havdalah – separation; a ceremony that marks the end of Shabbat and festivals. It is made over wine, spices and the light of a plaited candle.

Hazzan – cantor; a person who leads prayer using traditional tunes.

Kashrut – the Jewish dietary laws derived from Leviticus and Deuteronomy.

Kedusha – holiness, particularly bringing something of the holiness of God into the world.

Ketubah – the wedding document detailing the rights of the wife.

Kiddush – sanctification; a prayer that proclaims the holiness of Shabbat and festivals. It is recited before meals over a cup of wine.

Kosher – 'proper'; describes food fit to eat according to Jewish dietary laws.

Mezuzah – a small box nailed to the right-hand doorposts in a Jewish home, containing verses from Deuteronomy 6: 4–11 and 11: 13–21.

Minyan – quorum of ten adult males required for community prayer.

Ner Tamid – the eternal light found in the synagogue.

Noahide Code – seven commandments given to Noah for the whole of humanity; they are: worship only one God, don't blaspheme God, don't commit adultery, don't steal, don't commit murder, practise justice, be kind to animals.

Purim – holiday celebrating events described in the Book of Esther; occurs in February/March.

Rabbi – teacher; usually applied to any graduate from a seminary. Originally it applied to any wise teacher.

Seder – the meal on the first evening of Pesach.

Sefer Torah – the Torah scrolls, handwritten by a scribe called sefer.

Shofar – ram's horn trumpet.

Simhat Torah – the last day of the festival of Sukkot, which marks the end of the yearly readings from the Torah. It is a day of rejoicing and thanking God for the Torah.

Tallit – a prayer shawl worn by Orthodox Jewish men.

Tefillin – two small boxes, worn by Orthodox men, containing words from the Torah. One is bound to the forehead and the other to the left arm adjacent to the heart.

Torah – instructions or teaching; the first five books of the Tenakh.

Sikhism

Akhand Path – continuous reading of the Guru Granth Sahib from beginning to end.

Amrit Sanskar – initiation into the Khalsa.

Anand Karaj – the marriage ceremony.

Ardas – formal prayer that begins or ends every ritual. Its three parts encourage Sikhs to remember the Gurus, the teachings of the Guru Granth Sahib and to ask for God's blessing on the Sikh community and all peoples.

Avatar – the belief that God descends to earth to restore righteousness. Sikhs reject avatars.

Avidya – spiritual ignorance.

Baisakhi – the second month of the Hindu calendar; spring harvest festival in the Punjab, is celebrated by Sikhs in April to remember the forming of the Khalsa (the community of the pure).

Brahmins – priestly caste of Hinduism.

Dhoti – a piece of cloth wrapped around the loins. A traditional form of dress among Hindu men.

Diwali – a major Hindu festival celebrated in October–November. In 1577 the foundation stone of the Golden Temple was laid at Diwali, and Guru Harogobind was released from prison at Diwali in 1619.

Granthi – one who reads the Guru Granth Sahib. There is no priesthood in Sikhism. Although any member of the congregation can read from the book, the granthi plays a special role in caring for the Guru Granth Sahib.

Gurdwara – 'the doorway to the Guru'; a Sikh temple.

Gurmukh – God-centred or -oriented.

Gurmukhi – 'from the mouth of the Guru'; the written form of Punjabi used in the Sikh scriptures.

Guru Angad (1504–52) – the second Guru, ordained by Guru Nanak.

Guru Gobind Singh (1666–1708) – the tenth Sikh Guru and founder of the Khalsa (the community of the pure).

Guru Granth Sahib – Sikh holy scriptures.

Halal – meat that is killed and prepared in a way required by Muslims.

Harmandir Sahib – 'temple of God'; the Sikh temple in Amritsar which is sometimes called Darbar Sahib (Divine Court) and is commonly known as the Golden Temple.

Haumai – egoism; the major spiritual defect.

Hukam – 'divine order' or the will of God.

Janam Sakhis – 'life story' of Guru Nanak.

Japji – the first of Guru Nanak's shabads (hymns). A Sikh should recite the japji every morning.

Ka'bah – Muslim shrine in Makkah; Muslims believe it to be the first house built for the worship of the One True God.

Karma – in Hinduism the law of cause and effect which results in reincarnation.

Khalsa – the community of the pure; the Sikh community.

Khanda – double-edged sword used to stir amrit; also the symbol on the Sikh flag.

Kirat karna – earning one's living by honest means.

Kirtan Sohila – evening prayer; also read at funerals and when the Guru Granth Sahib is laid to rest.

Langar – Guru's kitchen; the gurdwara dining hall and the food served in it. Everyone, regardless of status, is welcome to stay for longer.

Lavan – marriage hymn composed by Guru Ram Das.

Maghi – Hindu month in which the winter solstice falls.

Manmukh – self-oriented (as opposed to gurmukh, God-oriented).

Maya – delusion; when the soul identifies itself with physical matter; to be wrong about what is truly real.

Mool Mantra – the basic statement of belief about God at the beginning of the Guru Granth Sahib.

Mukti – spiritually liberated.

Nam simran – keeping God constantly in mind.

Nishan Sahib – the Sikh flag flown outside a Gurdwara.

Panj Piare – 'the five beloved ones'; the first Sikhs to be initiated into the Khalsa; also refers to representatives of these first five who perform the initiation today.

Sat Guru – one true *Guru*.

Sat Nam – 'the true name'; a popular Sikh name for God.

Sewa – selfless service.

Vand chhakna – sharing one's time, talents and earnings with those less fortunate.

Waheguru – 'wonderful lord'; a popular Sikh name for God.

Index

Akhand Path 189, 198, 207, 209
Allah 105–7, 118
Amritsar 184, 189
Anglican 35, 53, 54, 61
ashramas (stages of life) 80–1
aum 69, 73, 98
avatars 71, 73, 93, 186, 187

baptism 38, 50–1, 54, 58
Bar/Bat Mitzvah 158
bhikkhus 26
bhikkunis 26
Bible 59–61, 117, 188
    (see also Gospels)
blessings 142, 144, 159
Brahma 69–70, 70, 93
Brahman 69–70, 74, 80
Brahmins 82, 87
Buddha (Siddhattha Gotama) 10–14, 24, 26, 28–31
    (see also Buddhism)
Buddhism 7, 9–10, 12–23, 26–7
    festivals 31–2
    worship 28–31
    (see also Buddha; Pali Canon)

calendars 74–5, 111, 172
caste system 82, 183, 191
Christ
    (see Jesus of Nazareth)
Christian Church 34–5, 45–8, 57, 60, 60–1
Christianity 7, 34–40, 61, 63–5, 104
    festivals 41, 55–7
    sacraments 50–3

worship 41, 45–8, 60–1
    (see also Bible; Gospels; Jesus of Nazareth)
Christmas 55–6
Church, Christian
    (see Christian Church)
circumcision 127, 156–7
commandments (mitzvot) 22, 139, 141–2, 146, 148, 162
Communion, Holy 51–3, 54, 58
communities
    Buddhist (Sangha) 27
    Muslim (ummah) 129, 131–3, 134
Communities
    Sikh (Khalsa) 191–4
creation 5, 36, 38, 40, 172, 175
cross (Christian symbol) 47–8, 58

dates 8, 56, 172
death 23–4, 90–1, 128–9, 133, 160–1, 205–6
denominations, Christian 35, 46–7, 48
dhamma (eternal truth) 7, 12
dhammachakra (dhamma wheel) 19
dharma (religious duty) 76, 80, 83
dietary rules
    Buddhism 27
    Hinduism 84, 85
    Islam 126
    Judaism 150, 152–3, 154
    Sikhism 202
dress 128, 134, 147, 163–4, 195

Index

Easter 51, 55, 56–7, 58
Eightfold Path 17–20
enlightenment 12, 14, 16
equality 34, 177
Eucharist 48, 51–3, 61

family life 126–7, 152–5,
    204–7
fasting (sawm) 121–2, 124
festivals
    Buddhist 31–2
    Christian 41, 55–7
    Hindu 75–7
    Islamic 126–9
    Jewish 146, 167–71
    Sikh 207–9
five Ks (Panj Kakkar) 182, 186,
    192, 194–7
five pillars of Islam 118–24
Five Precepts 20–3, 26
fonts 51, 54
food and drink
    (see dietary rules)
Four Noble Truths 14–17, 19
funerals 90–1, 128–9, 133,
    160–1, 205–6

Gandhi, Mahatma 82, 84, 86
Ganges, River (Ganga Ma) 91,
    95, 96, 97, 98
Gobind Singh, Guru (1666–
    1708) 186, 187, 191
God 7, 14
    Christianity 35–9, 56
    Hinduism 69–72
    Islam 105–7, 118
    Judaism 141–2, 161–2
    Sikhism 175–8
Golden Temple (Amritsar)
    184, 188, 190, 208
Gospels 41, 43, 61, 103, 109
Gotama, Siddhattha
    (see Buddha)
gurdwaras 174, 187, 189,
    197–201, 202, 208

Guru Granth Sahib (Sikh
    scriptures) 174, 175, 184,
    186, 188–91
    in ceremonies 192, 204,
    206
    in gurdwaras 197–201
Gurus, Sikh 174, 183–8

Hadith 107, 110, 113, 116
hajj (pilgrimage to Makkah)
    122–3, 125, 126
halal food 126, 202, 203
Hinduism (Sanatan Dharma) 7,
    68–9, 84–5, 95–7
    festivals 75–7
    God 69–72
    journey of life 79–80
    samskars 86–91
    scriptures 92–4
    worship 98–100
holiness (kedusha) 149–50,
    151
Holy Communion 51–3, 54,
    58
Holy Spirit 36–7, 39, 45, 51,
    57, 60
Holy Trinity 36–7, 39, 57
homes 98–9, 126–7, 130,
    152–5, 156
human nature 6, 37–8, 50, 142

icons 46, 48
Islam 7, 103–9, 136–7
    family life 126–7
    festivals 124, 126–9
    five pillars 118–24
    life rituals 126–9, 130
    worship 118–20, 124, 125,
    126, 132–3
    (see also Hadith; mosques;
    Prophet Muhammad
    (570–632); Qur'an)

jataka tales 24–5
Jesus of Nazareth 34, 43, 47–8,
    56–7, 63–4, 109

life 40–3, 42
    as Son of God 36, 39, 42–3, 55, 56
    teachings 43, 63–5
    (see also Christianity)
Judaism 6, 34, 104, 139–40, 148–50
    family life 152–5
    festivals 146, 167–71
    life rituals 156–61, 163
    worship 145–6, 163–7
    (see also Torah)
justice 149, 150

Ka'bah 110, 113, 122, 124
Kamma 21, 22
    (see also karma)
Karma 21, 81, 187
kasher foods 150, 152–3, 156
kashrut (Jewish dietary laws) 150, 152–3, 156
kedusha (holiness) 148–50, 163
Khalsa (community of the pure) 191–4
Krishna 71, 76–7

langar (communal kitchen) 180, 199, 201
life rituals 86–91, 126–9, 130, 156–61, 204–7
life stages (ashramas) 80–1, 201
love 38, 56, 63–4, 148–9

Makkah 110, 111, 112, 129
    direction for prayer 126, 132, 133
    hajj 122–3, 125, 126
marriages 86, 88–90, 127–8, 158–60, 201, 204–5, 206–7
mass 46, 48, 52
meditation 16, 19, 82
mezuzah 146, 150, 152
mitzvot (commandments) 22, 139, 141–2, 146, 148, 162

moksha (spiritual liberation) 79, 81, 95
monks, Buddhist 9, 10, 11, 22, 26, 27
mosques 107, 132–3, 134–5
Muhammad, Prophet
    (see Prophet Muhammad)
murtis (Hindu deity images) 28, 70, 73, 74, 98, 101

naming ceremonies 157–8, 204
Nanak, Guru (1469–1539) 174, 178–82, 201
New Year, Jewish 169–70
nibbana (nirvana) 7, 16, 17, 21

Orthodox Church 35, 46, 50, 55, 60–1

Pali Canon 23–4
Panj Kakkar
    (see five Ks)
Paschal candles 51, 54, 59
Pentecost 35, 45, 55, 57, 59
pilgrimages 95–7, 167
    hajj 122–3, 125, 126
prayers, Muslim (salah) 119, 124, 125, 132–3
Prophet Muhammad (570–632) 103, 113–14, 116, 118, 121, 128
    life 110–13
    (see also Islam)
prophets 36, 103, 109, 157, 162
    (see also Prophet Muhammad)
Protestant Churches 47–8, 50, 61
puja (Hindu worship) 75, 98–100

Qur'an 103, 109, 111–12, 114–15, 121, 125
    respectful treatment 114–15

Index

Rama 71, 93
Ramadan 111, 113, 121, 125
RE, aims 5–6
reincarnation 79, 95, 205
religions, role 6–7, 48, 116
resources
    Buddhism 33
    Christianity 67
    Hinduism 102
    Islam 138
    Judaism 173
    Sikhism 209
resurrection 56, 129
Roman Catholic Church 35,
    46–7, 50, 52, 60–1
rupa (Buddha images) 28–31

Sabbath (Shabbat) 153–4,
    164–5
sacraments 50–3
salah (five set daily prayers)
    119, 124, 125, 132
salvation 7, 14, 50, 52
samsara 21, 79, 82
samskars 86–91
Sanatan Dharma
    (see Hinduism)
Sangha (Buddhist community)
    10, 26–7
saptapadi 89–90
sawm (fasting) 121–2, 124
Shabbat (Sabbath) 153–4
Shahadah 105, 128
Shakti 72
Shema (prayer) 141, 149, 160
Shiva 70, 71–2, 75, 93
shruti 92
Siddhattha Gotama
    (see Buddha)
Sikhism 7, 174–8, 201–4
    festivals 207–9
    five K's 182, 186, 192,
        194–7
    life ceremonies 204–7
    worship 198–9

(see also Guru Granth
    Sahib; Gurus; Khalsa)
sin 7, 38, 39, 105, 113
smriti 93
stewardship 5
Sunnah 110, 116, 118, 129
syllabuses 5–6
synagogues 146, 158–60,
    163–7

temples, Hindu 98, 99–100,
    101
Tenakh (Hebrew Bible) 139,
    141, 145
time, Hindu view 74–5
tolerance 68
Torah 144, 144–6, 161, 164,
    165, 166
    affirmed by Muslims 103,
        109
Trinity, Holy 36–7, 39, 57
tzedakah (charity) 149, 151

ummah (Muslim community)
    129, 131–3, 134

varna (caste) system 82, 183,
    191
Vishnu 70, 70–1, 73, 93

wheel of life 79–80, 82, 95
women 127–8, 130, 177
worship
    Buddhist 28–31
    Christian 41, 45–8, 60–1
    Hindu 98–100
    Jewish 146
    Muslim 118–20, 124, 125,
        132–3
    Sikh 198–9
wudu (ablutions) 119–20, 124,
    133

yogas (spiritual paths) 80, 82,
    83

zakah (giving to the
    community) 120–1, 124

ra-za